Meal Prep

Fast and Easy Recipes for Weight Loss and Clean Eating

Clayton West

acknowledge that the author is not engaging in the rendering of legal, financial, medical or professional advice. The content of this book has been derived from various sources. Please consult a licensed professional before attempting any techniques outlined in this book.

By reading this document, the reader agrees that under no circumstances are is the author responsible for any losses, direct or indirect, which are incurred as a result of the use of information contained within this document, including, but not limited to, —errors, omissions, or inaccuracies.

Table of Contents

Introduction

In today's dynamic world, it is quite a challenge for most of us to make time for anything other than work. As a result, today's generation faces newer health hazards every other day. This sudden deterioration in health can primarily be attributed to our eating habits! We don't find the time to cook our meals anymore and take refuge in fast foods!

Studies have proven time and again, the harm that fast foods can cause to our bodies. Yet, we resort to these because they are easier to get and don't involve us spending hours in the kitchen! The very thought of spending an hour in the kitchen to just cook a paltry meal dissuades us.

What if I told you that you could cook your own meals in no time, if you spent few hours prepping them? I see that I have caught your attention! You will agree with me when I say that prepping takes a lot of time as opposed to actual cooking. But, you can save a lot of time if you prep for several meals at once. That's what meal prep is all about!

When you cook your own meals, there are countless benefits! Cooking your own meals can be a lifestyle change and a permanent solution to most of your health disorders. I am sure your motivation to cook will increase when you know that meal prep is easier than you thought!

Do not get discouraged if this is the first time you are hearing about this concept of prepping for your meals in advance. This book will be your go-to guide on meal prepping and will help you on your path towards clean eating.

I have addressed all crucial aspects of meal prepping in this book, starting from how it is done to why it is done, how to avoid some common mistakes etc. I have also provided several practical tips in this book, which can help you stay on track. There are also several exciting recipes in this book, which can help you come up with your diet plan!

Thank you for purchasing this book and I hope you find it useful!

Chapter 1: How to Meal Prep?

In this chapter, I have given an overview on how you can go about prepping your meals!

Come Up with a Plan

The first thing that you need to do is to come up with a diet plan. Take your time and come up with a meal plan for the week. When you have a solid diet plan, getting your ingredients, prepping for it and staying focused is a lot simpler.

If you are dieting for the first time and are fretting about coming up with a solid diet plan, do not worry. I have some exciting recipes listed in this book for you! I also have a chapter containing a sample diet plan, which you can make use of. If you are not so good at planning your meals, just sift through my recipes and pick the ones that you like for your plan. Another advantage of having a diet plan is that you can source ingredients in bulk and save money and time spent in multiple shopping trips.

Invest in Good Containers

It is extremely important that you invest in good food storage containers. Otherwise, all the time you spent prepping for the next week will go in vain. Make sure you buy containers to address the different ingredients that you are using. Certain ingredients stay fresh within an airtight box while others do so inside a glass jar. Do a bit of research and invest in good ones.

Stock Your Pantry

Once you have a diet plan, quickly scan your pantry and see what you need to buy. Go out and get all the requisite ingredients. Once you are back from the store, make sure you store the ingredients in appropriate containers for prepping later.

Pick a Prep Day

Choose a day of the week for prepping your ingredients. If you feel that you can accommodate more time for prepping, you can prep your food every 3 days. You should also be mindful about your refrigerator's capacity before you decide the day. If your refrigerator doesn't have enough capacity, you will not be able to prep for 5 or 6 days' worth meals in advance.

Prepping Ingredients

Each ingredient will have to be prepped in a different way. Here is how you prep for some of the frequently used ingredients:

Fruits: Wash them well and cut them up! If the core or seeds need to be removed, make sure you get rid of them.

Vegetables: Wash them well and cut them based on how you like them (ex: julienned, chopped etc.) To save more time, you can invest in a good spiralizer and finish your prepping in no time.

Chicken and meat: Shred or cube your chicken and store them in large containers in your refrigerator. You can also brown your meat and store it in the refrigerator.

Rice and pasta: Cook them and store it. They usually stay good for at least 3 to 5 days.

Make sure you store these ingredients in good containers and label the boxes. Since each ingredient has its own shelf life, labeling is important to know when you prepped the ingredient.

Chapter 2: Why it is Important to Meal Prep

Prepping your meals has several benefits, which aren't obvious. I have listed some of the important reasons for meal prep in this chapter.

Improves your Time Management

Most of us complain about not having time for various things, starting from cooking our meals to finishing our favorite book, from hanging out with friends to cleaning up our room. How does meal prep improve my time management when I hardly have any time? Well, that's where the magic comes in.

Spending time for prepping your meals is like an investment for a rainy day. When you prep your meals for the week, you no longer have to spend time worrying about your meals. You no longer have to go out to buy your dinner. When you reduce your intake of fast food and junk food, the amount of time spent to burn those extra calories and shed those extra pounds is saved. An added benefit is that you get to eat healthy meals and lose weight!

Helps you Stay Focused

How many of us have been thrilled about losing weight in the first week of dieting, only to find the enthusiasm tends to fade in the next few days? When you are planning to resort to clean eating for weight loss, it is extremely important that you focus on what and how much you eat.

Most often, we are discouraged by trying to figure out the nutritional content in what we eat outside of the home. Our lack of motivation is heightened when we realize that we can't find healthier options to eat out and we are no way near losing the weight we want to lose.

When you prep your meals, your problem of searching for nutritional ingredients is sorted out. Similarly, when you prep your meals, you can be sure about the nutritional content of your meals. You will be able to measure them out and ensure that you stick to your plan at all times.

Save Money with Prepping!

We often take refuge in the misconception that eating fast food is a cheaper option, as opposed to getting our own ingredients from the grocery store and cooking them. Like I just said a minute ago, it is a big misconception.

When you get your ingredients and prepare your own meals, you will actually end up saving a lot of money. Meal prepping also helps you save a lot of time. Still don't believe me? Next time you cook something, just list the price of each ingredient that you are using up. Compare it with the price that you would pay for the same dish at your favorite restaurant. You will be surprised by the considerable amount of money you would be saving.

Let's you Keep an Eye on the Portions

A balanced diet is all about consuming the right amount of nutrients. It has always been important that you follow a balanced diet. When you are dieting for weight loss, it is of paramount importance that you pay attention to what you eat. When you cook your own meals, you have the liberty to tweak the ingredients and their amount, to balance out the nutritional value.

For instance, if you had a lunch, which was heavy on

carbs, you can now adjust your dinner to ensure that your overall carb intake for the day stays the same. You will not have the same luxury when it comes to junk and fast food. We all know that fast foods do not carry the same nutritional value as home cooked meals. These little adjustments to your meals can help you stay on track.

Makes Shopping Easy!

Planning your meals is extremely important, especially if you want to save time. When you are in the habit of prepping for your meals for the week, you know for sure what you want to cook through the week. With that in mind, you know what ingredients you need. Going out grocery shopping has never been so easy.

This also helps you stay on track. How so? Imagine walking inside a superstore without a grocery list! You would be tempted to walk through the aisles containing all your favorite junk foods. When you are on a diet, it is important that you stay focused and not pile up on junk food. Having a grocery list helps you stay focused and also ends up saving a lot of time.

Dealing with Cravings

Cravings are the biggest distracters when you are on a diet. Most of us get through the breakfast and lunch courses pretty well. Where we start failing is when our cravings set in during the day. It would be so convenient to just grab a quick hotdog or a taco and be done with it.

But, what do we know about the nutritional content in these foods? I have already stressed enough about staying away from fast foods and junk foods, while you are dieting for weight loss. When you are prepping your own meals, you can prep something for your snacks as well. In fact, this book has some excellent snack recipes that can help you satisfy your sudden cravings.

Regulate Your Metabolism

Our metabolism gets messed up when we eat unevenly sized meals at odd times. This is also another reason why we put on weight easily. Making sure that you eat healthy meals at regular intervals will not only help you deal with your weight loss but also help you regulate metabolism.

When you diet, it is no longer about eating three or four heavy meals every six or seven hours. It is about having light meals every three or four hours. When you prep your meals, you are ready to handle your diet plan! Consuming light meals at frequent intervals also improves your metabolism.

Chapter 3: How to modify your Mindset to shed weight

Forget About Fear

Within the realm of weight-loss, fear will be bad as chocolate pudding. It's possible you'll fear searching for clothes, of taking photos, of just being simply embarrassed, the weighing scale or the doctor's appointment. You will likely retreat should you commence worrying almost everything. Now this fear, it is very real and hard to battle off. Rather of permitting the fear handle you, it will be possible to take charge of your fear.

This is when the idea of goal setting techniques makes the image. You don't need to set big goals each can be quite a smaller target. Establish targets which are achievable. These types of simple things like refraining from having chocolates for any week!

You need to set an actual along with an intellectual task on your own, something which could frighten you to create a sensible decision, mainly because decisions are method for accomplishing that target. Set up a challenge and also a timeline intended for conquering the challenge. This can keep you motivated to help keep going.

Fire Up the Current

You must have an optimistic mindset in case you really wish to shed every person excess kilos. Steady but very slow triumphs the competition. The options that you simply make during an amount of time will certainly determine how well you're progressing.

Change needs time to work also there is no such thing as overnight. This goes accurate with regard to going on a diet. It isn't just about altering your diet plan you'll have to toss in something in to the mix in case you really wish to achieve unwanted weight goal.

You'll be effective at possessing an eating plan only when the diet plan doesn't seem like a consequence for you. You need to benefit from the experience what sort of kid would certainly take pleasure in recess. Enjoy activities that capture your imagination.

The consequence of genuinely committing yourself in anything is that you'll be capable of finding that which you were searching for with no additional effort and hard work. Continue to keep trying brand new quality recipes, diet does not imply boring food. Continue to keep things fascinating. On days whenever you long for something you shouldn't eat you are able to develop cheat snacks to satisfy your cravings. Don't consider the diet plan like a punishment, consider it as a way to some healthier existence.

Reversing the Leadership Model

People who wish to slim down fall under two groups typically. The very first category includes individuals who seem to desire to fight the fight independently and seclude their selves. The 2nd category includes the would-be person talking to and hearing the nutritionist, physician, trainer, the writer or perhaps the commercial merchant prior to staying on an eating plan. There's no problem with either from the models plus individuals can equally perform.

The issue pops up only if the follower will get fed up with following instructions. When you are fed up with following strict rules, you'll give to one's own cravings. However, the problem lies using the dieters.

What's needed is really a well-balanced plan involving following and leading. You'll have to get back a few of the control you've got unconsciously forwarded to professionals. There is no need to make a move mainly because that's exactly what your nutritional expert requested you to definitely do.

You have to recognize that you're following a diet for your own personal good and never with regard to another person. It is important to have confidence in your cause.

Chapter 4: Practical Tips to Make Meal Prepping Easy

I have enumerated some practical tips in this chapter, which will make meal prepping a lot easier. As such, prepping your meals helps saving a lot of time. With these tips, you will be able to save even more time!

Stick to Your Grocery List!

Once you have your diet plan in place, you will know the exact amount of ingredients that you will need. Stick to your shopping list. As I said before, it can be extremely satisfying to just toss a couple of chips packets onto your cart. But it is important that you stay focused.

Make sure that you avoid picking any junk foods while you are at the grocery store. Even if you managed to get something on the cart, have the resolve to say no to it before you cash out.

Don't Forget the Smoothie!

I have listed some amazing and delicious smoothie recipes in one of the following chapters for you to make use of. If you realize that your meals don't have enough fruits and vegetables in them, make yourself a smoothie. Having a smoothie also keeps you full for a long time and can help you keep your cravings at bay. The smoothies that I have mentioned in the subsequent chapter are pretty low on calories as well. So, you can have more than one during the course of the day!

Stick to Simple Snacks

It is important that you stick to simple snacks, especially if you don't want to spend a lot of time prepping. Go for snacks and meals that don't require a lot of time. When you choose simple snacks, you will also be able to prep for a lot of food in a short span of time. When you have enough food prepped, the chances of staying on track are high. Also, if you plan carefully, you can consume several low calorie snacks during the day. This will keep you energized through the day.

Try to Cook Everything at Once

When you are trying to cook several ingredients for the various mains or side dishes for the week, try doing it at once. For instance, if your recipes for the week involve you roasting sweet potatoes, potatoes, chicken breasts etc., make sure you cook them all in your oven at the same time.

This will save the time that you would have spent trying to cook the several ingredients separately. This approach also helps you consume less electricity while cooking the various ingredients, thus resulting in a lower electricity bill! In other words, more money saved!

Look for Easier Options

If your recipe permits and if you can source from healthier stores, go for ingredients that are already prepped. For instance, if you can get your hands on vegetables, which are pre-cut, you will be able to save more prep time. Go for ingredients that require minimal cooking time.

For instance, tuna is a beautiful protein that can be consumed raw. When you go for such ingredients, you can reduce your prep time as well as your cooking time. Similarly, look for cooking shortcuts that can help you cook several ingredients at the same time. As we already saw above, trying to get done several things at once can help you save a lot of time and energy.

Mix and Play Around

I know how excited you must be when you come up with your meal plans. Following the plans can be a bit difficult because we might get bored down the line. That's when fast food and junk foods start looking interesting to us! That is how you steer away from your diet plan!

To keep things interesting, try coming up with at least 2 lunch and dinner options for your meals. This way, you can choose the option that interests you most. You will no longer be tempted by fast foods and you will be more than motivated to stick to your diet.

Use an Oven to Hard Boil Eggs

Eggs are rich in proteins and should definitely form part of your everyday meal in some form or the other. The easiest way to cook an egg is to hard-boil it. Typically, you would use a pot to boil it. But that can boil only up to 4 to 5 eggs at a time. If you want to boil a batch of eggs, your oven can help you! Just arrange the eggs on a muffin tray and toss it inside the oven. Let it cook for 30 minutes. Say hello to your batch of boiled eggs! This way, you don't have to constantly stay near the stove to take out the boiled eggs, toss in the new ones etc.

Go for Salad Jars

I used to dread taking salads from home for lunch, mainly because of how soggy they used to get! And then I found this magic called glass jars! When you arrange a salad neatly inside a glass jar, it stays fresh for a long time and doesn't get soggy.

Get yourself a bunch of glass jars, if you can't get hold of salad jars that come with a separate compartment for dressing. First, pop in the dressing. This will be the bottom layer of your salad. Move on to arranging firmer vegetables like peppers, cucumbers etc., next. Top it with other ingredients such as leaves, nuts, quinoa etc.

If you are not going to use the salad immediately, just cover the ingredients with a paper towel. This will absorb the moisture and ensure that your salad stays fresh for days.

Chapter 5: Mistakes to Prevent

The most popular mistakes that individuals make when doing food preparation and slimming down are discussed within this chapter.

Staying Away from Salt

You have to have a little salt you shouldn't cure it. You are able to avoid headaches, weakness as well as muscle cramps to eat just a little salt when bodies are shifting coming from burning off carbs to fat meant for producing energy. However, you need to reduce your sodium absorption should you suffer from hypertension or if you've been recommended to do this from your physician.

Refusing to Eat Sufficient Protein

You will have to consume approximately four to six oz. of protein for every meal, based upon how old you are, gender and height. Four ounces may be enough for any petite lady however a man may need as much as 6 ounces. This does not imply that you ought to eat just protein and miss veggies, eat an excessive amount of protein or the other way around. This will hinder unwanted weight loss and you'll be also exposed to serious urges for carbohydrates.

Becoming Present the Weighing Scale

You need to weigh and measure your body one time each week. Unwanted weight has a tendency to effortlessly differ as much as four pounds in one day-to another. You'll you need to be in for failure should you frequently weigh on your own. This can simply trigger frustration as well as disappointment.

It's also likely that your muscle building and getting rid of fat while exercising. This may also result in a slight putting on weight and it is perfectly okay. So, your weighing scale may say you have gain pounds whereas you could just be wearing muscle whilst your garments start out turning out to be loose.

Overlooking to Capture How Well You're Progressing

You should record how well you're progressing. Conserve

a diary in which you can enter all of your weekly records relating to your measurements and weight. Tracking how well you're progressing can help you result in the appropriate modifications for your diet in order that it might fit your metabolic process well.

Being Frightened of Fat

There are specific nutritional fats which are required for your system to lose body fat which natural fats are good when you're conscious of the carb intake. It is best to eat a munch of carbs with both protein and fat.

Skipping Veggies

People should not be thrifty on vegetables. Make certain that 75% of the minimum carb consumption comes from vegetables. Therefore, you need to get your meals a minimum of two cups of cooked vegetables and as much as 6 cups of leafy vegetables on a daily basis.

Saying No Thanks to Water

It's important to drink a minimum of 8 glasses of water

each day which can improve your physical activity. As lengthy as the urine is pale or obvious, it signifies that you're consuming adequate water. 2 cups could be by means of broth or sugar-free drinks, tea or coffee. Perhaps it's a misguided attempt should you conserve money on water simply to visit a lower score around the weighing machines. Should you not take in enough water, the body will begin retaining water like a preventive measure.

Consuming Hidden Carbs

Browse the product labels on manufactured food items carefully. Due to the fact the package states low-calorie, don't think that this means reduced carb too. Make certain that you're using full fat variations of mayonnaise, bandages and similar items. The reduced-fat versions have a tendency to increase the sugar to exchange the taste that's put in by oil.

Chapter 6: Frequently Asked Questions

As a beginner, I am sure you must be having so many questions about meal prepping. I have compiled some of the frequently asked questions about meal prepping in this chapter.

Do I Refrigerate or Freeze my Meals? How Do I Go About Reheating Them?

If you are not planning to consume the meal for at least the next 3 days, then freezing your meals would be the ideal solution. This will ensure that the food doesn't get spoilt and remains fresh for a longer duration. The night before you intend to consume your meal, move it from the freezer to the refrigerator. This will allow the food to thaw overnight. Next morning, just pop the food into your microwave and reheat!

On the other hand, if the food is for consumption in the next couple of days, you can store your food in the refrigerator. Before you consume it, just add a touch of seasoning and herbs and reheat in the microwave.

Is it Fine to Freeze All my Meals?

34

Unfortunately, not all meals can be frozen. For instance, fruits and vegetables that have high water content and leafy vegetables turn soggy when you freeze them. Similarly, when you freeze your pasta, it can become a mushy mess when you let it thaw. Here is a list of some food items that cannot be definitely frozen.

- Hard cooked eggs or eggs in their shells
- Egg based sauces
- Fruits and vegetables with high water content
- Cultured dairy
- Soft cheeses

How Frequently Should I Prep my Meals?

I would recommend you prep meals for at least 4 to 5 days in advance. That way, you can save a lot of time.

Don't you get Bored by Eating the Same Thing Every Week?

It doesn't necessarily have to be boring! You can plug and play around with your recipes. Since you have everything prepped, you can customize when you cook by adding more condiments or vegetables. Plus, I have mentioned several recipes in this book, so there is no room to get bored!

Chapter 7: Four Week Meal Plan

Day 1

Breakfast - <u>Bacon, Avocado and Jack Cheese Omelet with Salsa</u>

Lunch - <u>Roasted Red Pepper Soup</u>

Snack - <u>Baked Asparagus Fries</u>

Dinner - <u>Bahian Halibut</u>

Desserts - <u>Chocolate Peppermint Cupcakes</u>

Day 2

Breakfast - <u>Beef Huevos Rancheros</u>

Lunch - <u>Bacon and Goat Cheese Salad</u>

Snack - <u>Jalapeño Cornbread Muffins</u>

Dinner - <u>Beef Coconut Curry</u>

Desserts - <u>Chilled Lemon Cheesecake</u>

Day 3

Breakfast - <u>Fried Eggs and Vegetables</u>

Lunch - <u>Rainbow Salad</u>

Snack - <u>Sweet Potato Hummus</u>

Dinner - <u>Asian Tuna Kebabs</u>

Desserts - <u>Chocolate Squares</u>

Day 4

Breakfast - <u>Bacon and Egg Casserole</u>

Lunch - <u>Mexican Chicken</u>

Snack - <u>Baked Parmesan Zucchini</u>

Dinner - <u>Greek Salad with Grilled Chicken Breast</u>

Desserts - <u>Frozen Yogurt Popsicles</u>

Day 5

Breakfast - <u>Scrambled Tofu</u>

Lunch - <u>Cauliflower – Curry Soup</u>

Snack - <u>Potato Chips</u>

Dinner - <u>Broiled Spicy Orange Chicken Breasts</u>

Desserts - <u>Flan</u>

Day 6

Breakfast - <u>Egg Muffins</u>

Lunch - <u>Avocado Zucchini Soup</u>

Snack - <u>Healthy Cookie Dough Peanut Butter Protein Balls</u>

Dinner - <u>Eggplant Gratin</u>

Desserts - <u>Pineapple Coconut Granita</u>

Day 7

Breakfast - <u>Baby Spinach Omelet</u>

Lunch - <u>Ground Beef and Spinach Skillet</u>

Snack - <u>Baked Asparagus Fries</u>

Dinner - Cheddar Cheese Open Sandwiches

Desserts - Fruit Salad

Day 8

Breakfast - Pumpkin Pancakes

Lunch - Chicken Salad

Snack - Orange Glazed Carrots

Dinner - Zucchini Bread

Desserts - Chilled Lemon Cheesecake

Day 9

Breakfast - Tropical Fruits Smoothie

Lunch - Borlotti bean and Kale Soup

Snack - Jalapeño Cornbread Muffins

Dinner - Asparagus, Mushrooms & Peas

Desserts - Decadent Chocolate Ice Cream

Day 10

Breakfast - Banana Pancakes

Lunch - Cauliflower "Mashed Potatoes"

Snack - Sweet Potato Hummus

Dinner - Grilled Steak with Salsa

Desserts - Chocolate Squares

Day 11

Breakfast - Apple Muffins with Cinnamon - Pecan Streusel

Lunch - Asian Tuna Kebabs

Snack - Parmesan Crusted Scalloped Potatoes

Dinner - Spicy Tofu Lettuce Wrap Tacos

Desserts - Chocolate Peppermint Cupcakes

Day 12

Breakfast - Egg muffins

Lunch - Warm Salad

Snack - Super Seed Crackers

Dinner - Avocado Salad with Walnuts

Desserts - Frozen Yogurt Popsicles

Day 13

Breakfast - Californian Breakfast Burrito

Lunch - Mexican Chicken

Snack - Potato Chips

Dinner - Ground Beef and Spinach Skillet

Desserts - Pineapple Coconut Granita

Day 14

Breakfast - Low Carb Porridge

Lunch - Cheddar Cheese Open Sandwiches

Snack - Baked Asparagus Fries

Dinner - Eggplant Gratin

Desserts - Flan

Day 15

Breakfast - Chocolate Peanut Butter Smoothie

Lunch - Asian Beef Salad with Edamame

Snack - Tomato Soup

Dinner - Chicken Kebabs

Desserts - Chilled Lemon Cheesecake

Day 16

Breakfast - Bacon and Egg Casserole

Lunch - Beef Coconut Curry

Snack - Orange Glazed Carrots

Dinner - Creamy Cheesy Bake

Desserts - Chocolate Squares

Day 17

Breakfast - Almond Soy Mini Muffins

Lunch - Mexican Chicken

Snack - Baked Parmesan Zucchini

Dinner - Spicy Tofu Lettuce Wrap Tacos

Desserts - Pineapple Mango Layer Cake

Day 18

Breakfast - Scrambled Tofu

Lunch - Ground Beef and Spinach Skillet

Snack - Healthy Cookie Dough Peanut Butter Protein Balls

Dinner - Grilled Steak with Salsa

Desserts - Fruit Salad

Day 19

Breakfast - Atkins Cuisine Bread

Lunch - Garlic Potatoes

Snack - Parmesan Crusted Scalloped Potatoes

Dinner – Zucchini Bread

Desserts - Frozen Yogurt Popsicles

Day 20

Breakfast - Acorn Squash with Spiced Applesauce and Maple Drizzle

Lunch - Red Cabbage Slaw with Mustard Vinaigrette

Snack - Easy Garlic Parmesan Knots

Dinner - Cream of Chicken Soup

Desserts - Decadent Chocolate Ice Cream

Day 21

Breakfast - Granola Parfait

Lunch - Bacon and Mushroom Chicken

Snack - Baked Asparagus Fries

Dinner - Zucchini Pasta Salad

Desserts - Pineapple Coconut Granita

Day 22

Breakfast - Mexican Potato Omelet

Lunch - Chicken Pasta Soup

Snack - Sweet Potato Hummus

Dinner - Soya Bean and Peas Soup

Desserts - Flan

Day 23

Breakfast - Apple Muffins with Cinnamon - Pecan Streusel

Lunch - Cheddar Cheese Open Sandwiches

Snack - Super Seed Crackers

Dinner - Cauliflower "Mashed Potatoes"

Desserts - Pineapple Mango Layer Cake

Day 24

Breakfast - All Purpose Low Carb Baking Mix

Lunch - Spicy Tofu Lettuce Wrap Tacos

Snack - <u>Sweet Potato Hummus</u>

Dinner - <u>Ground Beef and Spinach Skillet</u>

Desserts - <u>Chocolate Squares</u>

Day 25

Breakfast - <u>Almond Pancakes</u>

Lunch - <u>Japanese Vegetables and Tofu Soup</u>

Snack - <u>Healthy Cookie Dough Peanut Butter Protein Balls</u>

Dinner - <u>Mexican Chicken</u>

Desserts - <u>Frozen Yogurt Popsicles</u>

Day 26

Breakfast - <u>Pineapple Almond Milk Smoothie</u>

Lunch - <u>Asian Tuna Kebabs</u>

Snack - <u>Super Seed Crackers</u>

Dinner - <u>Beef Coconut Curry</u>

Desserts - <u>Fruit Salad</u>

Day 27

Breakfast - <u>Dairy free latte</u>

Lunch - <u>Chicken Kebabs</u>

Snack - <u>Potato Chips</u>

Dinner - <u>Warm Salad</u>

Desserts - <u>Chilled Lemon Cheesecake</u>

Day 28

Breakfast - Cheesy Tuna Casserole

Lunch - Greek Salad with Grilled Chicken Breast

Snack - Herbed Quinoa

Dinner - Grilled Steak with Salsa

Desserts - Pineapple Coconut Granita

Day 29

Breakfast - Breakfast Chocolate Smoothie

Lunch - Spicy Tofu Lettuce Wrap Tacos

Snack - Sweet Potato Hummus

Dinner - Cauliflower "Mashed Potatoes"

Desserts - Chocolate Squares

Day 30

Breakfast - Bell Pepper Rings filled with Egg and Mozzarella

Lunch - Cheddar Cheese Open Sandwiches

Snack - Baked Parmesan Mushrooms

Dinner - Eggplant Gratin

Desserts - Chocolate Peppermint Cupcakes

Chapter 8: Breakfast Recipes

Bacon, Avocado and Jack Cheese Omelet with Salsa

Serves: 8

Ingredients:

- 8 large eggs
- 2 tablespoons butter, unsalted
- 6 slices bacon, cooked, crumbled
- 2 cups Monterey Jack cheese, shredded
- 2 ounces of water

For Salsa:
- 1 large ripe tomato, chopped
- 1 jalapeño pepper, finely chopped
- 1 avocado, peeled, pitted, chopped
- 6 medium spring onions, finely chopped
- 2 tablespoons fresh lime juice
- 2 tablespoons fresh cilantro, chopped
- Salt to taste
- Pepper powder to taste

Instructions:

1. To make salsa: Mix together all the ingredients of the salsa and set aside.

2. Whisk together eggs, water, salt and pepper.

3. Place a nonstick skillet over medium heat. Add 1/2-tablespoon butter. When the butter melts, add 1/4 of the egg mixture. Lightly swirl the pan so that the egg spreads.

4. Cook until nearly set. Sprinkle 1/4 each of bacon, avocado and cheese over one half of the omelet. Fold the other half over it. Remove on to a plate and serve.

5. Repeat steps 3 and 4 with the remaining egg mixture and filling.

Scrambled Eggs

Serves: 4

Ingredients:

- 8 large eggs
- 2 tablespoons heavy cream
- Salt to taste
- Pepper powder to taste
- 2 teaspoons fresh parsley, chopped
- 1 teaspoon fresh tarragon, chopped
- 1 tablespoon unsalted butter

Instructions:

1. Whisk together eggs, cream, salt, pepper, tarragon, and parsley.
2. Place a nonstick skillet over medium heat. Add butter.
3. When the butter melts, add the egg mixture. Cook for a minute. Then scramble it with a wooden spoon. When the eggs are soft and creamy, remove from heat and serve immediately.

Beef Huevos Rancheros

Serves: 6

Ingredients:

- 6 large eggs
- 9 ounces of lean ground beef
- 6 slices Canadian bacon
- 3/4 cup canned green chili pepper
- 1 1/2 teaspoons chili powder
- 1/2 teaspoon garlic powder
- 1/2 teaspoon ground cumin
- Salt to taste
- Pepper to taste
- 1/2 teaspoon dried oregano
- 3/4 cup cheddar cheese, shredded
- 2-3 tablespoons fresh cilantro, chopped
- Cooking spray

Instructions:

1. Place a skillet over medium heat. Spray with cooking spray. Add beef and cook until brown.

2. Add chilies, garlic powder, chili powder, cumin, oregano, salt and pepper and cook for another 5-7 minutes.

3. Place the bacon slices on top of the beef and remove from heat.

4. Place a skillet over medium heat. Spray with cooking spray. Add eggs, cook until lightly set and scramble it.

5. To serve: Place a slice of bacon on each plate. Divide the beef mixture into 6 portions and place over the bacon.

6. Divide the scrambled eggs and place over the beef.

7. Sprinkle cheese and cilantro and serve.

Fried Eggs and Vegetables

Serves: 4

Ingredients:

- 8 eggs, beaten
- 2 tablespoons extra-virgin olive oil
- 1 cup cauliflower florets, chopped into small pieces
- 1 cup broccoli florets, chopped into small pieces
- 2 cup spinach, thinly sliced
- Salt to taste
- Pepper to taste
- 1/2 teaspoon chili powder
- 1 teaspoon dried oregano

Instructions:

1. Place a nonstick skillet over medium high heat. Add oil. When the oil is heated, add cauliflower and broccoli and sauté for 3-4 minutes.
2. Add eggs, salt, pepper, chili powder and oregano and stir.
3. Add spinach and stir until the eggs are cooked.
4. Serve hot.

Cheesy Tuna Casserole

Serves: 4

Ingredients:

- 3 cans (6 ounces each) tuna, drained
- 24 ounces frozen chopped French green beans, cooked according to instructions on the package
- 5 ounces of fresh mushrooms, chopped,
- 2 stalks celery, finely chopped
- 3 tablespoons onion, finely chopped
- 3 tablespoons butter
- 3/4 cup chicken broth
- 1 cup heavy cream or more if required
- Salt to taste
- Pepper powder to taste
- Xanthan gum (optional)
- 8 ounces of cheddar cheese, shredded

Instructions:

1. Place a skillet over medium heat. Add butter. When butter melts, add onions and sauté for a couple of minutes. Add mushrooms and celery and sauté until light brown.

2. Add broth and boil until the broth reduces in quantity by half. Reduce heat and simmer until thick. Stir frequently.

3. Add salt, pepper, tuna, beans and the sautéed mushrooms to a casserole dish.

4. Top with cheese. Bake in a preheated oven at 325° F until the cheese is melted and bubbling.

Baby Spinach Omelet

Serves: 4

Ingredients:

- 8 eggs, whisked well
- 4 cups baby spinach, torn
- 6 tablespoons parmesan, grated
- 1 teaspoon onion powder
- 1/2 teaspoon ground nutmeg
- Salt to taste
- Pepper powder to taste
- Cooking spray

Instructions:

1. Add eggs, spinach, and cheese, nutmeg, salt, pepper and onion powder to a bowl and mix well.
2. Place a nonstick pan over medium heat. Spray with cooking spray.
3. Pour the egg mixture and cook until almost set and the underside is golden brown.
4. Flip sides and cook the other side too.
5. Serve hot.

Egg Muffins

Serves: 10

Ingredients:

- 10 large eggs, beaten
- 1 medium green bell pepper, diced
- 3/4 cup low fat cheddar cheese
- 3 tablespoons feta cheese
- 1 teaspoon garlic seasoning or to taste

Instructions:

1. Add beaten eggs, green pepper, and garlic seasoning to a bowl and whisk well.
2. Grease muffin molds. Pour the egg mixture (3/4 full) into the muffin molds.
3. Bake in a preheated oven at 325° F for 25-30 minutes or until the muffins are set and browned.
4. Serve hot. They can last for a week if refrigerated.

All Purpose Low Carb Baking Mix

Serves: 4

Ingredients:

- 1/2 cup crude wheat bran
- 10 ounces of vanilla whey protein powder
- 10 ounces of vital wheat gluten
- 2 1/4 cups whole grain soy flour
- 1/2 cup whole ground golden flaxseed meal

Instructions:

1. Mix together all the ingredients and store in an airtight container. Refrigerate until use. It can store up to a month.

Atkins Cuisine Bread

Serves: 8

Ingredients:

- 2 cups + 1 tablespoon Atkins cuisine all-purpose baking mix - refer to recipe 11 further down
- 1 1/2 tablespoons baking powder
- 1/2 teaspoon salt
- 1 packet granular sugar substitute
- 18 tablespoons cold water
- 3 tablespoons vegetable oil

Instructions:

1. Mix together all the dry ingredients in a large bowl.
2. Add water and oil. Use a spatula mix well to form a dough.
3. Take out the dough from the bowl using the spatula and place on a lightly greased, clean work area.
4. Coat your hands with a little oil. Using your hands shape the dough as desired.
5. Place the dough into a greased bread pan.

6. Bake in a preheated oven at 350° F   for 1 hour or until done.

7. Remove from oven and place on a wire to cool.

8. Slice only when cooled completely and serve. Store unused bread in an airtight container.

Californian Breakfast Burrito

Serves: 6

Ingredients:

- 6 low carb tortillas, warmed according to the instructions on the package
- 12 large eggs, beaten
- 5 spring onions, thinly sliced
- 1 1/2 tablespoons canola oil
- 6 ounces canned green chili peppers
- 3 tablespoons fresh cilantro, chopped
- 1 large tomato, chopped
- Salt to taste
- Pepper to taste
- 1/4 teaspoon cayenne pepper
- 3/4 cup cheddar cheese, shredded
- Fresh salsa to serve - refer 1st recipe

Instructions:

1. Place a nonstick skillet over medium high heat. Add oil. When the oil is heated, add green onions, tomatoes, salt and pepper and sauté for a couple of minutes.

2. Add eggs and cayenne pepper and stir. Cook until the eggs are done until the consistency you desire. Remove from heat.

3. Place the tortillas on your work area. Divide and place the egg mixture on the tortillas. Sprinkle cilantro and cheese. Add about a tablespoon of fresh salsa.

4. Roll and serve.

Almond Pancakes

Serves: 4

Ingredients

- 1 ¼ cups almond meal
- 4 eggs, separated
- 1 teaspoon baking powder
- Splenda to taste
- 2 tablespoons butter
- ½ teaspoon salt

Instructions:

1. Whisk together in a bowl, yolks, cream, and Splenda until creamy.
2. Whisk the whites in another bowl until soft peaks are formed.
3. Mix together ground almond and baking and add to the yolk mixture. Whisk well until there are no lumps.
4. Add about 1/4 the whites into the mixture and whisk.

5. Add rest of the whites and fold gently.

6. Place a pan over medium flame. Add about 1/2 tablespoon butter. When butter melts, add about 1/4 of the batter over the pan at the center. Swirl the pan around so that the batter spreads.

7. Cook until the underside is golden brown. Flip sides and cook the other side too.

8. Repeat the above 2 steps with the remaining batter.

9. Serve warm.

Bacon and Egg Casserole

Serves: 4

Ingredients

- 3 strips of bacon
- 4 large eggs
- 2 tablespoons green bell pepper
- 1 small onion, chopped
- 4 mushrooms, chopped
- 1/2 cup cheddar cheese
- 4 tablespoons ground flaxseeds
- 1/2 teaspoon salt or to taste
- 1/2 teaspoon pepper powder
- 1/2 teaspoon dried thyme
- 1/3 cup soy milk, unsweetened
- 1 tablespoon olive oil

Instructions:

1. Place a skillet over medium heat.
2. Add oil. When the oil is heated, add onions, pepper,

and mushrooms and sauté until onions are translucent.

3. Transfer into a greased baking dish. Spread all over the dish.

4. Layer with cheese followed with bacon.

5. Whisk together eggs, milk, ground flaxseed, thyme, salt and pepper.

6. Pour over the vegetables in the baking dish.

7. Bake in a preheated oven at 350° F   until the center begins to set.

8. Switch off the oven and let the dish remain in the oven for 10 minutes before serving.

Almond Soy Mini Muffins

Serves: 12

Ingredients:

- 1 cup unsalted butter, softened
- 1 1/2 cups granulated Splenda
- 1 teaspoon vanilla extract
- 6 eggs
- 1 cup ground almond
- 1 cup soy flour
- 6 teaspoons cinnamon powder
- 1 teaspoon baking powder
- 1/2 teaspoon salt

Instructions:

1. Mix together all the dry ingredients in a large bowl.
2. In another bowl, add butter, vanilla and sweetener. Whip until light and fluffy.
3. Gradually add eggs one by one and beat well.
4. Add the dry ingredients, a little at a time and fold gently.

5. Spoon the batter into lined mini muffin pans (keep it 3/4 full).

6. Bake in a preheated oven at 350° F for about 18-20 minutes or until a toothpick when inserted in the center comes out clean.

Low Carb Porridge

Serves: 4

Ingredients:

- 4 cups coconut or almond milk
- 4 tablespoons sunflower seeds
- 4 tablespoons chia seeds
- 4 tablespoons flaxseeds, whole or crushed
- 1/4 teaspoon salt
- 1 teaspoon ground cinnamon
- Fresh berries to serve
- Butter to serve

Instructions:

1. Place a saucepan over medium heat. Add all the ingredients except berries and butter. Stir and bring to the boil.
2. Lower heat and simmer for 2-3 minutes.
3. Remove from heat and serve with butter and berries

Scrambled Tofu

Serves: 4

Ingredients:

- 2 tablespoons olive oil
- 2 bunches green onions, chopped
- 2 cans (14.5 ounce each) peeled, diced tomatoes along with the juice
- 2 packages (12 ounces each) firm silken tofu, drained, mashed
- 1/2 teaspoon ground turmeric
- Salt to taste
- Pepper powder to taste
- 1/2 teaspoon red chili flakes
- 1 cup cheddar cheese, shredded (optional)

Instructions:

1. Place a skillet over medium heat. Add oil. When the oil is heated, add green onions. Sauté until tender.
2. Add turmeric, salt and pepper. Sauté for about a minute.
3. Add tofu and tomatoes along with the juice. Mix well.
4. Lower heat and let it heat thoroughly. Sprinkle cheddar cheese if using, and serve.

Acorn Squash with Spiced Applesauce and Maple Drizzle

Serves: 4

Ingredients:

- 2 acorn winter squash (4 inches of diameter each), deseeded, chopped into wedges
- 1 1/2 cups apple sauce, unsweetened
- 4 tablespoons butter, unsalted
- 1/4 teaspoon ground cinnamon
- 2 tablespoons sugar free maple syrup
- 1 teaspoon salt
- 1 teaspoon pepper powder

Instructions:

1. Line a baking dish with foil.
2. Melt about 2 tablespoons of butter and brush the squash with it. Season with salt and pepper and place on the baking dish.
3. Bake in a preheated oven at 350° F for about 18-20 minutes or until tender.

4. Meanwhile, add applesauce to a pan and heat it over low flame. Add remaining butter and cinnamon and cook until well blended.

5. Remove from heat.

6. Serve squash with applesauce. Drizzle a little maple syrup and serve.

Pumpkin Pancakes

Serves: 8

Ingredients:

- 6 large eggs, beaten
- 1/3 cup whole grain soy flour
- 1/3 cup blanched almond flour
- 6 ounces of vanilla whey protein
- 1 1/2 teaspoons baking powder
- 1/3 cup curd cream cottage cheese
- 3/4 cup canned pumpkin puree, unsalted
- 3/4 teaspoon pumpkin pie spice
- Butter or canola oil to make pancakes

Instructions:

1. Mix together in a bowl, all the dry ingredients.
2. Add egg, curd cream cottage cheese and pumpkin puree and stir until well combined.
3. Place a nonstick pan over medium heat. Add a little butter. When the butter melts, pour about 1/4 cup of batter on the pan. Slightly swirl the pan for the

batter to spread.

4. Cook until the underside is golden brown. Flip sides and cook the other side too. Remove from the pan and keep warm.

5. Repeat steps 3 and 4 with the remaining batter.

6. Serve warm.

Apple Muffins with Cinnamon - Pecan Streusel

Serves: 12-15

Ingredients:

- 4 large eggs, beaten
- 3 1/3 cups almond flour
- 4 tablespoons high fiber coconut flour
- 4 tablespoons butter, unsalted, melted
- 1 cup pecans, chopped
- A large pinch stevia
- 16 tablespoons erythritol
- 1/2 cup coconut milk, unsweetened
- 2/3 teaspoon salt
- 4 teaspoons vanilla extract
- 2 teaspoons baking powder
- 1 1/3 cup apple, peeled, cored, finely chopped
- 5 tablespoons ground cinnamon

Instructions:

1. To make pecan streusel: Mix together in a bowl, 1 1/3 cup almond flour, pecans, 4 tablespoons cinnamon, 1/4 teaspoon salt, small pinch stevia, 4 tablespoons erythritol and butter. Mix until a crumbly texture is formed and set aside.

2. To make muffins: Add eggs, coconut milk, vanilla, 12 tablespoons erythritol, small pinch erythritol, and remaining cinnamon to a bowl and whisk well.

3. Add remaining almond flour, coconut flour, remaining salt, and baking powder and mix until well combined.

4. Add apples and fold gently.

5. Pour into lined muffin tins. (Fill up to 1/2). Sprinkle about 2 tablespoons streusel over it.

6. Bake in a preheated oven at 350° F for about 22-25 minutes.

7. Cool for a while and serve.

Bell Pepper Rings filled with Egg and Mozzarella

Serves: 4

Ingredients:

- 4 large eggs
- 1/2 cup mozzarella cheese, shredded
- 1 kiwi fruit, peeled, chopped
- 1/2 cup raspberries
- 1 large banana, sliced
- 1 small apple, cored, chopped
- 1 medium or large bell pepper, sliced into 4 rings of 1 inch each
- 1 tablespoon extra-virgin olive oil

Instructions:

1. Place a skillet over medium high heat. Add oil. When the oil is heated, add the bell pepper rings.
2. Break an egg into each of the ring and cook for a couple of minutes.
3. Add about 2 tablespoons water and cook until the egg is set until the softness you desire is achieved.

4. Sprinkle cheese and remove from heat. Cover and set aside for a minute.

5. Meanwhile mix together all the fruits and place on 4 individual serving plates. Place an egg with ring in each plate and serve.

Granola Parfait

Serves: 4

Ingredients:

- 2 cups plain, low fat yogurt
- 2 cups fruits or berries of your choice
- Artificial sweetener or stevia drops to taste
- 1/4 cup rolled oats
- 3/4 cup nuts, chopped
- 2 tablespoons seeds of your choice, toasted
- 1/2 tablespoon olive oil
- 1/2 teaspoon cinnamon
- 1/4 teaspoon vanilla extract
- A pinch of salt

Instructions:

1. In a large bowl mix together the oats, nuts, olive oil, cinnamon, vanilla, salt and a little sweetener.
2. Spread evenly on a greased baking dish.
3. Bake in a preheated oven at 350° F   for around 45 minutes, stirring it every 15 minutes.

4. The granola should be golden brown if not then bake further for another 10-15 minutes.

5. To serve: Spoon in the yogurt into glasses. Add some sweetener and stir.

6. Next layer it with fruits and then granola.

7. Repeat the layer. Sprinkle seeds on top.

8. Chill and serve later.

Mexican Potato Omelet

Serves: 3

Ingredients:

- 6 large eggs, well beaten
- 1 1/2 tablespoons olive oil, divided
- 1 red potato (4-5 ounces), rinsed, scrubbed, halved, thinly sliced
- 2 cloves garlic, finely chopped
- 1 cup tomatoes, chopped
- 2 green onions, thinly chopped
- 1/4 teaspoon sea salt or to taste
- 1/4 teaspoon pepper powder or to taste
- 1/3 cup pepper Jack cheese
- 2 tablespoons fresh cilantro, chopped
- 1/2 teaspoon fresh lime juice

Instructions:

1. Add half the oil to a broiler proof skillet and place over medium low heat.

2. Add potatoes, cover and cook until golden brown. Stir occasionally. Add garlic, most of the scallions, salt and pepper and sauté for about a minute.

3. Add the remaining oil to the pan.

4. Meanwhile, add 1/4-cup tomatoes and 1/4-cup cheese to the eggs and mix well. Pour over the potatoes and cook until the center is almost done.

5. Sprinkle remaining tomatoes, scallions, cilantro, lime juice and cheese over it.

6. Broil in a preheated broiler for 2-3 minutes.

7. Cut into wedges and serve with salsa.

Banana Pancakes

Serves: 8

Ingredients:

- 1 cup almond milk or soy milk
- 4 eggs
- 3 tablespoons butter + extra butter for frying the pancakes
- 2 tablespoons gluten free baking powder
- 2 bananas, pureed
- 1 1/2 cups coconut flour
- 1/2 cup brown rice flour

Instructions:

1. In the food processor bowl, whisk together milk, eggs, and 3 tablespoons butter. Mix well.
2. Add baking powder, coconut flour, rice flour, and bananas until smooth.

3. Heat a non-stick griddle pan over medium heat. Add about a teaspoon of butter. When the butter melts, pour the batter to make small pancakes. Cook until the underside is golden brown. Flip sides and cook the other side too.

4. Serve warm or hot.

Chapter 9: Lunch / Dinner Recipes

Cream of Chicken Soup

Serves: 4

Ingredients:

- 4 stalks chopped celery
- 1 teaspoon dried parsley
- Salt to taste
- White pepper powder to taste
- 4 cups chicken broth
- 2 tablespoons dehydrated minced onions
- 1 cup chopped cooked chicken
- 4 cloves minced garlic
- 1 teaspoon dried basil

Instructions:

1. Add all the ingredients to a food processor and pulse until the consistency you desire is achieved.

2.   Place a saucepan over medium high heat. Pour the blended mixture into the saucepan and bring to the boil.

3.   Lower heat, cover and simmer for about 20 minutes.

4.   Serve in soup bowls.

Borlotti bean and Kale Soup

Serves: 3

Ingredients:

- 1 cup chopped curly kale
- Salt to taste
- Pepper powder to taste
- 2 tablespoons Parmesan, shredded (optional)
- Crusty bread (optional)
- 1/2 tablespoon olive oil
- 1 medium cut into small chunks potato
- 1/2 tablespoon tomato puree
- A few sprigs fresh thyme
- 1 bay leaf
- 2 1/2 cups chicken or vegetable stock
- 1 cup drained, rinsed canned Borlotti beans
- 1 small peeled, diced onion
- 1 medium carrot, peeled, diced

Instructions:

1.   Place a pan over medium heat. Add oil. When the oil is heated, add carrots and onions and sauté for 3-4 minutes.

2.   Add bay leaf, potato, tomato puree and thyme. Sauté for a couple of minutes and add the stock.

3.   Bring to the boil. Reduce heat and simmer for about 10 minutes, cover the pan partially.

4.   Add pepper, beans and salt. Increase the heat back to medium and bring the soup to a boil.

5.   Add kale on top; cook until kale wilts.

6.   Serve in soup bowls sprinkled with Parmesan with crusty bread if using.

Greek Salad with Grilled Chicken Breast

Serves: 6

Ingredients:

- 2 medium chopped cucumbers
- 3 medium chopped ripe tomatoes
- 1 1/2 cups crumbled feta cheese
- Cooking spray
- 30 ounces of skinless chicken breasts
- 9 cups shredded romaine lettuce
- 3/4 cup sliced red onions
- 18 pitted black olives

For dressing:

- 4 teaspoons water
- 3 teaspoons dried oregano
- 1/2 teaspoon salt
- Pepper powder to taste
- 5 tablespoons red wine vinegar
- 1/3 cup extra virgin olive oil
- 1 clove minced garlic

Instructions:

1.   Sprinkle pepper and salt over chicken and set aside for a few minutes.

2.   Whisk together all the ingredients of the dressing and set aside.

3.   Preheat a grill. Spray chicken with cooking spray and grill the chicken breasts on both the sides until cooked. Remove from the grill, cover and set aside.

4.   Add the remaining ingredients of the salad in a bowl. Pour half the dressing and toss well.

5.   Divide and place the salad on individual serving plates. Place chicken breasts on top. Pour the remaining dressing over the chicken and serve.

Asian Beef Salad with Edamame

Serves: 3

Ingredients:

- 1 teaspoon ground ginger
- 1 tablespoon canola oil
- 1 1/2 cups spring mix salad
- 1 small chopped into strips red bell pepper
- 4 ounces of water chestnuts
- 1 cup shelled edamame
- 2 scallions or spring onions
- 1/2 teaspoon minced garlic
- 1 tablespoon tamari sauce
- 1/2 teaspoon rice vinegar
- 1/2 teaspoon toasted sesame oil
- 1/4 teaspoon Splenda
- 9 ounces trimmed of fat beef top sirloin
- 1/4 teaspoon curry powder

Instructions:

1. Add to a bowl, green onions, garlic, tamari sauce, rice vinegar, sesame oil, and Splenda. Mix well.

2. Pour half of this into a zip lock plastic bag. Keep the remaining half aside.

3. To the zip lock bag, add steak and marinate for 7-8 hours in the refrigerator.

4. Place a large skillet over high heat. Add canola oil. When the oil is very hot, remove beef from the zip lock bag and add to the skillet. Fry until the beef is cooked. Transfer into a large serving bowl.

5. Add mixed greens, bell pepper, water chestnuts, and edamame and mix well.

6. To the other half of the sauce that was kept aside, add curry powder and ginger.

7. Pour this over the salad. Toss well and serve.

Kale Salad

Serves: 6

Ingredients:

- 1 head kale
- 2 cups mixed greens
- 2 peeled and diced cucumbers
- 4 peeled, pitted, diced avocados
- 4 tomatoes, diced
- 2 cans drained and rinsed garbanzo beans (chickpeas)
- Topping: hemp seeds or sunflower seeds

For dressing:

- 1 cup tahini
- 1 1/2 cups water + more if required
- 1/4 cup lemon juice
- 2 cloves garlic, minced
- Salt to taste
- Pepper powder, to taste

Instructions:

1. To make the dressing: Add all ingredients of the dressing to a bowl. Whisk well.

2. Add the salad ingredients to a bowl. Pour the dressing over it. Mix well.

3. Chill and serve later.

Garlic Potatoes

Serves: 3-4

Ingredients:

- 12 medium sized red or Yukon gold potatoes, rinsed, chopped into small cubes with skin on
- 1/4 cup olive oil
- 1 cup soy or almond milk
- Salt to taste
- Pepper powder to taste
- 5 cloves garlic, minced
- 1/3 cup nutritional yeast (optional)

Instructions:

1.   Place the potatoes in a large saucepan filled with water. Place the saucepan over high heat and bring to a boil. Cook until the potatoes are tender. Drain the water and place the potatoes in a large bowl.

2.   Add rest of the ingredients and mash well and serve with Atkins bread.

Roasted Red Pepper Soup

Serves: 3

Ingredients:

- 1/3 cup heavy cream
- 1 cup water
- 2 tablespoons grated parmesan cheese
- Salt to taste
- Pepper powder to taste
- 8 ounces roasted bell peppers
- 1 stalk chopped celery
- 1 cup cooked chopped into bite size pieces of chicken
- 4 teaspoons extra virgin olive oil
- 2 cups chicken broth
- 2 cloves minced garlic
- 1 small chopped onion

Instructions:

1. Place a saucepan over medium heat. Add in oil. When the oil is heated, add garlic, celery, onions and

sauté until soft.

2. Add water, roasted peppers and stock and bring to the boil.

3. Reduce heat and simmer for 5-6 minutes.

4. Remove from heat and cool for a while. Blend with an immersion blender. Pour the soup back into the saucepan.

5. Reheat the soup. Add pepper, cream, salt and stir. Heat for a couple of minutes more.

6. Serve in soup bowls garnished with cheese.

Cauliflower - Curry Soup

Serves: 4

Ingredients:

- Pepper to taste
- 2 inch pieces grated ginger
- 1 tablespoon extra-virgin olive oil
- 2 small finely chopped onion
- 1 tablespoon curry powder
- 4 cloves minced garlic
- 1 cup heavy cream
- 4 tablespoons fresh chopped chives
- Salt to taste
- 2 small head cut into small florets cauliflower
- 2 cups vegetable broth
- 2 cups water

Instructions:

1.   Place a saucepan over medium heat. Add oil. When the oil is heated, add onions and sauté until translucent. Add ginger, curry powder, garlic and sauté until fragrant.

2.   Add water, cauliflower and broth. Bring to a boil.

3.   Lower heat, cover, and cook until the cauliflower is tender.

4.   Add cream. Mix well and remove from heat. Blend the soup with an immersion blender.

5.   Pour the soup back to the saucepan and reheat. Add pepper and salt. Heat thoroughly and serve in soup bowls garnished with chives.

Avocado Zucchini Soup

Serves: 4

Ingredients:

- 1/2 teaspoon salt
- Pepper powder to taste
- 1 chopped Hass avocado
- 2 tablespoon lemon juice
- 2 tablespoon chopped red bell pepper
- 2 tablespoons extra-virgin olive oil
- 4 chopped, divided green onions
- 2 teaspoon grated ginger root
- 2 garlic clove, chopped
- 30-ounce vegetable broth
- 1 cup water
- 2 thinly sliced zucchinis

Instructions:

1.   Place a large saucepan over medium heat. Add olive oil. Leaving aside 1 tablespoon of the green onion, add the

rest to the saucepan. Sauté for 2-3 minutes.

2.   Add ginger and garlic. Sauté for a couple of minutes until fragrant. Add pepper, vegetable broth, water, zucchinis and salt.

3.   Cover and cook for a while until the zucchinis are tender. Remove from heat and let it cool for a while.

4.   Add avocado. Blend the soup in a blender or with an immersion blender. Transfer the soup back to the saucepan. Reheat the soup and once done, remove from heat.

5.   Add lemon juice and red bell pepper. Mix well. Sprinkle the retained green onions.

6.   Serve in soup bowls.

Zucchini Pasta Salad

Serves: 4

Ingredients:

- 1/3 cup parmesan, grated
- Salt to taste
- Pepper powder to taste
- 1 teaspoon lemon zest, grated
- 3 tablespoons olive oil
- 2 medium yellow zucchinis
- 2 medium green zucchinis
- 2 tablespoons lemon juice

Instructions:

1.   Make noodles of the zucchinis using a spiralizer or julienne peeler.
2.   Add all the ingredients to a large bowl and toss well.

Tuna Salad with Capers

Serves: 4

Ingredients:

- 8 chopped into bite size pieces boiled eggs
- 8 finely chopped leeks
- Salt to taste
- Pepper powder to taste
- Chili flakes to taste
- 1 cup of mayonnaise
- 4 cans drained tuna fish in water
- 4 tablespoons capers
- 8 tablespoons sour cream

Instructions:

1. Add all the ingredients to a bowl and toss well.
2. Serve!

Bacon and Goat Cheese Salad

Serves: 6

Ingredients:

- 3 tablespoons red wine vinegar
- 1-2 large beaten eggs
- 2 tablespoons Dijon mustard
- 8 cups shredded romaine lettuce
- 1 teaspoon black pepper powder or to taste
- Salt to taste
- 3 servings Atkins cuisine bread, made into crumbs
- 4 tablespoons chopped chives
- 4 cups chopped endives
- 16 ounces of soft goat cheese, cut into slices
- 12 medium slices bacon
- 4 tablespoons extra virgin olive oil

Instructions:

1.   Place a nonstick skillet over medium heat. Add bacon and cook until crisp. Remove with a slotted spoon and place on paper towels. Crumble when cooled.

2.   Retain about 2 tablespoons of the bacon fat and discard the rest.

3.   Place bread crumbs on a plate.

4.   Dip the goat cheese slices in the egg, one at a time (shake off the excess egg) and dredge in the breadcrumbs.

5.   Place the nonstick skillet back on heat. Add a little oil and cook the cheese slices in batches on both the sides until brown. Remove with a slotted spoon and place on paper towels.

6.   Meanwhile make the dressing as follows: Add the retained bacon fat, pepper, remaining olive oil, vinegar and mustard powder to the skillet and whisk well.

7.   Place the bacon and greens to a salad bowl. Pour the dressing over the salad and toss well.

8.   Divide the salad and place on individual plates. Place a goat cheese patty on each plate and serve.

Rainbow Salad

Serves: 6

Ingredients:

- 1 cup shredded red cabbage
- 1 cup torn lettuce
- 2 thinly sliced radishes
- 1 cup cubed fresh mozzarella cheese
- 2 cups baby carrots, chopped into bite size pieces, blanched
- 2 cups cooked whole wheat pasta
- 1 cup chopped, divided basil
- 1 cup shredded cabbage
- 2 large tomatoes
- 3 tablespoons olive oil

For balsamic dressing:

- 2 ounces of olive oil
- 2 ounces of white balsamic vinegar
- 2 teaspoons prepared mustard

- Salt to taste
- Pepper to taste

Instructions:

1.   Add all the ingredients of the dressing to a jar. Close the lid and shake vigorously and set aside.

2.   Add pepper, salt and a little olive oil to mozzarella. Mix well and set aside for a while.

3.   Add rest of the ingredients except remaining olive oil and half the basil to a large bowl.

4.   Pour dressing and toss well.

5.   Place the marinated mozzarella over the salad. Drizzle remaining olive oil over it. Garnish with remaining basil and serve.

Warm Salad

Serves: 4

Ingredients:

- 2 cups sliced new potatoes
- 4 quartered radishes
- 16 halved cherry tomatoes
- 2 tablespoons olive oil
- 1 cup sliced haloumi cheese

For the dressing:

- 2 tablespoons Dijon mustard
- 8 tablespoons chopped fresh dill
- Salt to taste
- Pepper to taste
- 8 tablespoons extra virgin olive oil
- 2 tablespoons red wine vinegar

Instructions:

1.   Cook the potatoes in boiling water with 1/2-teaspoon salt added to it. When cooked, drain and set aside.

2.   Mix together olive oil, vinegar, Dijon mustard, and dill in a large bowl. Add the pepper, boiled potatoes, radishes, tomatoes and salt. Toss well.

3.   Heat a nonstick frying pan with oil. Add haloumi and cook on both the sides until golden brown.

4.   Add haloumi to the salad and mix. Divide into individual serving plates.

Mexican Chicken

Serves: 3

Ingredients:

- A large pinch black pepper powder
- 1 clove garlic
- 1/2 tablespoon taco seasoning
- Cheddar cheese for garnishing
- Sour cream for garnishing
- 1 tablespoon butter
- 1 1/2 boneless, skinless, cut into strips, chicken breasts
- 1/2 chopped into 1 inch cubes green pepper
- 1/2 chopped into 1 inch cubes red pepper
- 1 1/2 tablespoon lime juice
- 1 teaspoon dried onion
- 1 teaspoon cumin powder
- 1 tablespoon chicken broth
- 1/8 teaspoon red chili powder

Instructions:

1.   Mix together chili powder, lime juice, broth, cumin powder and dried onions in a bowl.

2.   Add the chicken strips and toss well.

3.   Place a nonstick skillet over medium heat. Add butter.

4.   When butter melts, add the taco seasoning, chicken pieces, red and green peppers, garlic and pepper powder. Stir.

5.   Cook until the chicken is tender.

6.   Transfer on to a microwavable serving platter and top with cheddar cheese. Microwave for about 30 seconds or until the cheese melts.

7.   Drizzle sour cream on top and serve.

Japanese Vegetables and Tofu Soup

Serves: 4

Ingredients:

- 1 medium shredded carrot
- 2 stalks sliced green onion
- 1 tablespoon chopped fresh cilantro
- 3 tablespoons Japanese tamari soy sauce
- Salt to taste
- Pepper to taste
- 4 ounces of firm chopped into small cubes tofu
- 4 cups vegetable broth
- 1 1/2 cups chopped bok choy
- 1 1/2 cups sliced mushrooms
- 1 medium chopped tomato
- 2 teaspoons ginger, garlic
- 1 deseeded, minced Serrano pepper
- 1 clove sliced garlic

Instructions:

1.   Place a saucepan over medium heat. Add broth and soy sauce and bring to the boil.

2.   Add garlic, bok choy, mushrooms, ginger and Serrano pepper and bring to the boil.

3.   Lower heat, cover and simmer for about 5 minutes.

4.   Add carrot, tomatoes, green onions, tofu and heat thoroughly.

5.   Add cilantro and stir.

6.   Serve hot in soup bowls.

Chicken Pasta Soup

Serves: 4

Ingredients:

- 4 cups fat free chicken broth
- Pepper to taste
- Salt to taste
- 1/2 cup whole wheat rotini pasta
- Cooking spray
- 1 chicken breast (6 ounces), skinless, boneless, chopped into bite sized pieces
- 1/2 cup cut into matchsticks carrots
- 1 medium chopped onion
- 2 stalk chopped celery
- 1 chopped bell pepper

Instructions:

1.   Place a saucepan over medium heat. Spray with cooking spray. Add bell peppers, chicken, onions, celery, carrots and sauté until the vegetables are tender.

2.   Add pasta and broth and bring to the boil.

3.   Lower heat and cook until pasta is al dente.

4.   Serve hot in soup bowls.

Red Cabbage Slaw with Mustard Vinaigrette

Serves: 4

Ingredients:

- 1 1/2 pound shredded red cabbage
- 2 teaspoons grated lemon zest

For dressing:

- 2 teaspoons prepared mustard
- 3 tablespoons granulated sweetener
- 4 tablespoons extra virgin olive oil
- 2 teaspoons finely minced onion
- 1/2 cup rice vinegar

Instructions:

1. Add all the ingredients of the dressing to a salad bowl and whisk until well combined.
2. Add cabbage and toss well.
3. Cover and refrigerate for a couple of hours.
4. Garnish with lemon zest and serve.

Avocado Salad with Walnuts

Serves: 4

Ingredients:

- 4 cut into strips spring onions
- Juice of half a lemon
- 10 tablespoons mayonnaise
- Mixed leaves salad to serve
- 4 rashers of smoked bacon
- 4 cut into strips lengthwise sticks celery,
- 2 skinned, diced avocado
- 4 tablespoons chopped walnuts

Instructions:

1. Preheat a grill. Grill bacon on a wire rack until the bacon is crisp.
2. Mix together lemon juice, celery, avocado, walnuts and spring onions. Add mayonnaise. Toss well.
3. Arrange the salad leaves on a serving platter. Place the salad mixture at the center of the plate.
4. Garnish with bacon and serve.

Creamy Cheesy Bake

Serves: 6-8

Ingredients:

- 2 pounds frozen or fresh broccoli, boiled, drained
- 4 ounces of butter
- Salt to taste
- Pepper powder to taste
- 2 teaspoons garlic powder
- 1 large head chopped into small florets cauliflower
- 3 shredded cups cheese
- 16 ounces of cream cheese
- 1 cup heavy whipping cream

Instructions:

1.   Add garlic powder, cream cheese, cream, salt and pepper to the boiled broccoli. Blend with an immersion blender until smooth.

2.   Grease a baking dish with a little butter. Make small cubes of the remaining butter and place all over the

dish.

3.   Place the cauliflower florets in the baking dish. Pour the pureed broccoli mixture over the cauliflower.

4.   Sprinkle cheese all over the dish.

5.   Bake in a preheated oven at 350°F until the cauliflower is tender and the top is golden brown.

Eggplant Gratin

Serves: 8

Ingredients:

- 8 ounces of feta cheese
- 3 thinly sliced yellow onions
- 1 1/2 cups heavy whipping cream
- 1 1/2 tablespoons dried mint
- Salt to taste
- Pepper powder to taste
- 3 pounds of eggplants, cut into 1/2-inch-thick slices
- 3/4 cup grated cheese
- 3 tablespoons olive oil or butter
- 1/3 cup finely chopped parsley

Instructions:

1.   Brush olive oil on both the sides of the eggplant slices and place on a lined baking tray.

2.   Bake in a preheated oven at 400°F until golden brown.

3.   Place a skillet over medium heat. Add oil. When the

oil is heated, add onions and sauté until golden brown. Add salt and pepper. Stir and remove from heat.

4.   Grease a baking dish with a little oil. Place half the eggplant slices all over the bottom of the dish. Sprinkle half the parsley, onions, mint and about half the feta cheese.

5.   Place another layer of eggplant slices and remaining half of the onions. Sprinkle feta cheese and grated cheese. Finally spread whipping cream all over the cheese.

6.   Bake at 450°F for about 30 minutes or until the top is brown.

Grilled Steak with Salsa

Serves: 4

Ingredients:

- 1/2 teaspoon salt
- 1 1/2-pound flank steak or round
- Fresh salsa to serve - <u>refer 1st recipe in Chapter 8</u>
- Cooking spray
- 2 tablespoons ground cumin
- 4 cloves minced garlic
- 4 tablespoons lime juice
- 1 teaspoon black pepper powder

Instructions:

1.　　Pre-heat a grill or broiler rack.

2.　　Place a skillet over medium heat. Spray the skillet with cooking spray.

3.　　Add cumin and sauté until fragrant. Transfer into a bowl. Add garlic, 1-tablespoon lime juice, salt and pepper mix well.

4.   Rub this mixture on to the steak well on both the sides.

5.   Place in the grill and grill for 5 minutes per side or until cooked.

6.   Remove from the grill and cool slightly.

7.   Slice the steak into thin slices and serve with salsa.

Asian Tuna Kebabs

Serves: 3

Ingredients:

- 20 ounces of boneless tuna
- 1/2 pound chopped into chunks eggplant
- 1 medium chopped into 1 1/2 inches squares red bell pepper
- 2 large quartered scallions
- 2 teaspoons minced garlic
- 2 teaspoons minced ginger
- 2 ounces of rice wine
- 1 teaspoon sucralose based sweetener
- 2 teaspoons toasted sesame oil
- 3 tablespoons tamari or soy sauce
- Salt to taste

Instructions:

1.   Soak bamboo skewers in water for 15 minutes before grilling.

2.   Preheat a grill to high.

3.   Mix together in a bowl sucralose, ginger, garlic, soy sauce, rice wine, sesame, ginger and garlic. Add red bell, tuna, scallions and pepper. Mix well and set aside to marinate for 15 minutes in the refrigerator.

4.   Remove the tuna, scallions and bell pepper from it and thread on to the skewers along with the eggplant in any manner you desire and discard the marinade.

5.   Grill for about 3-4 minutes and serve.

Asparagus, Mushrooms & Peas

Serves: 6

Ingredients:

6 tablespoons unsalted butter

2 cups water

4 tablespoons heavy cream

2 tablespoons shredded parmesan cheese

1 cup peas

2 teaspoons minced garlic

6 ounces Portobello mushroom caps

6 medium sliced spring onions

1/2 cup apple cider vinegar

2 pounds of asparagus

A handful basil

Salt to taste

Pepper to taste

Instructions:

1.   Place a skillet over medium heat. Add 4 tablespoons butter. When the butter melts, add green onions and cook until it wilts.

2.   Add garlic and sauté until fragrant.

3.   Add remaining butter and mushrooms and cook until mushrooms are tender.

4.   Add vinegar and cook for a couple of minutes.

5.   Add water and asparagus and bring to the boil. Simmer for 2 minutes.

6.   Add peas and simmer until the peas are tender.

7.   Add cream and simmer until thick.

8.   Remove from heat. Sprinkle Parmesan and serve immediately.

Zucchini Bread

Serves: 15-18 slices

Ingredients:

- 1 teaspoon baking powder
- 1 cup canola oil
- 8 large eggs
- 2 medium zucchini, grated
- 2 teaspoons vanilla extract
- 2 cups almonds, finely ground
- 2 cups soy flour
- 2 cups granular sugar substitute
- 3 teaspoons ground cinnamon
- 1 teaspoon ground nutmeg
- 1 teaspoon salt
- 1 teaspoon baking soda

Instructions:

1. Mix together all the dry ingredients in a large bowl.

2. In another bowl, vanilla extract, add eggs, oil and zucchini. Whisk well. Pour this mixture into the dry mixture bowl. Mix well until the batter is well combined.

3. Transfer the batter into a generously greased bread pan.

4. Bake in a preheated oven at 370° F for about 35 minutes or until a knife comes out clean when inserted

5. Remove from the oven. Cool for 10 minutes and remove from the pan.

6. When cool enough to handle, slice and serve.

Broiled Spicy Orange Chicken Breasts

Serves: 6

Ingredients:

- 3 pounds skinless, quartered chicken breast
- Salt to taste
- Ground black pepper to taste

For marinating:

- 2 teaspoons Splenda sweetener
- 2 teaspoons orange rind, grated
- Cayenne pepper to taste
- 1/2 cup fresh orange juice
- 4 teaspoons minced garlic
- 2 tablespoons olive oil
- 2 tablespoons chili powder or to taste

Instructions:

1.   Sprinkle salt and pepper over the chicken.

2.   Mix together all the ingredients of the marinade. Add chicken and mix well.

3.   Transfer the entire contents to a large zip lock plastic bag. Refrigerate for a minimum of 8-7 hours.

4.   Preheat a broiler. Place the broiler rack such that it is about 6 inches away from the heating element.

5.   Remove from the refrigerator about 30 minutes before broiling.

6.   Broil the chicken for about 12-15 minutes or until done. Turn the chicken once while it is cooking.

Spicy Tofu Lettuce Wrap Tacos

Serves: 8

Ingredients:

- 1/2 teaspoon ground cumin
- 1/2 teaspoon ground ancho chili
- 1 ripe peeled, pitted, finely chopped avocado
- 1 head iceberg lettuce
- Fresh salsa to serve - refer to 1st recipe in chapter 6
- 8 ounces extra firm tofu, frozen, thawed, pressed of excess moisture, crumbled
- 2 tablespoons tamari or soy sauce
- 2 teaspoons creamy peanut butter
- 1/2 teaspoon garlic powder
- 1 teaspoon hot sauce

Instructions:

1.   Add chili powder, peanut butter, soy sauce, cumin, garlic powder and hot sauce to a microwave safe bowl and microwave for 20 seconds.

2.   Remove and mix well. Add tofu and stir.

3.   Transfer onto a greased baking sheet.

4.   Bake in a preheated oven at 350° F   for about 20 minutes.

Soya Bean and Pea Soup

Serves: 4

Ingredients:

- 2 cup light soy milk
- A handful of salad rocket leaves
- 1 cup frozen edamame beans (soya beans)
- 1 cup frozen peas
- 2 cup hot vegetable stock
- 6 trimmed, chopped spring onions
- 1 a small bunch basil leaves

Instructions:

1.   Place a saucepan over medium heat. Add spring onions, soya beans, peas and stock. Bring to the boil. Simmer for 5 minutes

2.   Add soymilk, basil and rocket leaves. Bring to the boil and remove from heat.

3.   Blend half the soup. Pour the blended soup back into the saucepan. Mix well and reheat.

4.   Serve hot in soup bowls.

Chicken Salad

Serves: 4

Ingredients:

- 10 tablespoons mayonnaise
- Freshly ground black pepper to taste
- Salt to taste
- 4 cups of chicken, finely shredded
- 6 tablespoons golden raisins, soak in warm water for about 10 minutes, drained
- 4 tablespoons chopped fresh chives
- 4 medium grated carrot

Instructions:

1. Add all the ingredients to a bowl and mix well.
2. Serve!

Bacon and Mushroom Chicken

Serves: 4

Ingredients:

- 1 tablespoon fresh parsley
- 1 1/2 teaspoons salt or to taste
- 1 pound mixed salad greens
- 1 tablespoon melted butter
- 4 smoked bacon
- 8 tablespoons whipped cream
- 20 quartered mushrooms
- 2 tablespoons chopped dill
- 2 cloves minced garlic
- 4 chicken breasts with skin

Instructions:

1.   Grease a baking dish with butter.

2.   Sprinkle dill, salt, garlic and parsley on both sides of the chicken. Place chicken in the baking dish.

3.   Place bacon over the chicken followed by a layer of mushrooms

4.   Bake in a preheated oven at 350°F for 45 minutes.

5.   Pour juices from the baking dish into a bowl. Add cream to it and mix.

6.   Pour it over the chicken.

7.   Serve chicken with mixed salad greens.

Bahian Halibut

Serves: 2

Ingredients:

- 1/2 teaspoon minced garlic
- 1/4 cup thick coconut milk or coconut cream
- 1/2 teaspoon salt
- 1 pound Atlantic and Pacific halibut
- 1 tablespoon extra-virgin olive oil
- 1/2 cup chopped green sweet pepper
- 1 small chopped onion
- 1 small chopped tomato
- 1 deseeded, chopped Serrano pepper
- 1 tablespoon lime juice

Instructions:

1.   Mix together 1/2-tablespoon oil and lime juice. Dip the fish in it and place on a platter. Set aside.

2.   Place a nonstick skillet over medium heat. Add Serrano pepper, garlic, onion and bell pepper. Sauté until the onions are translucent.

3.   Season fish with salt and place the fish in the skillet. Add tomatoes and coconut milk and stir.

4.   Lower heat and simmer until the fish is cooked.

5.   Taste and adjust the salt if needed. Serve immediately.

Ground Beef and Spinach Skillet

Serves: 3-4

Ingredients:

- ½ teaspoon chili pepper flakes
- A large pinch Himalayan salt
- A large pinch ground white pepper
- 1/2 cup pitted Kalamata olives
- 2 tablespoons capers
- 2 tablespoons natural roasted almond butter
- 3/4-pound baby spinach leaves, roughly chopped
- 4 tablespoons coconut oil or ghee
- 2 king chopped oyster mushrooms
- 4 tablespoons chopped raw almonds
- 3/4-pound grass fed ground beef

Instructions:

1.   Place a heavy bottomed skillet over medium high heat. Add ghee or oil. When the oil is melted, add

mushrooms and sauté until brown.

2.   Add almonds and sauté for a minute. Add white pepper powder, chili pepper flakes, beef and salt and cook until the meat is brown and cooked well.

3.   Add olives, capers and almond butter. Mix well. Add spinach and sauté for a couple of minutes until the spinach is cooked.

4.   Serve immediately.

Cheddar Cheese Open Sandwiches

Serves: 4

Ingredients:

- 8 ounces of thinly sliced sharp cheddar
- Salt to taste
- Pepper to taste
- 8 slices lightly toasted Atkins cuisine bread
- 2 tablespoons olive oil
- 1 medium thinly sliced red onion
- 2 tablespoons balsamic vinegar
- 1 teaspoon granular sugar substitute (sucralose)

Instructions:

1. Place a skillet over medium heat. Add oil. When the oil is heated add onions. Sauté until the onions are light brown.

2. Add pepper, balsamic vinegar, sugar substitute and salt. Mix well.

3. Lay the cheese slices over the bread. Divide the onion mixture over the cheese. Spread well.

4. Place in a preheated broiler, 4 inches from the heat source and broil until the cheese melts. Serve hot.

Chicken Kebabs

Serves: 6

Ingredients:

For the Kebabs:
- 1/2 teaspoon ground cumin
- Salt to taste
- Freshly ground pepper to taste
- 6 chicken fillets, de skinned, cut into chunks
- 1/2 cup low carbohydrate yogurt
- 3 teaspoons ginger paste
- 1/2 teaspoon ground turmeric
- 1/2teaspoon ground coriander

For the Dip:
- 3 tablespoons lime juice
- 1 1/2 teaspoon curry paste
- 1/2 cup low carbohydrate yogurt
- 1/3 cup crunchy peanut butter
- 3 tablespoons soy sauce

Instructions:

1.   Mix together all the ingredients of the kebab except chicken and mix well. Add chicken. Coat the chicken with the marinade. Set aside for at least a couple of hours. The longer the better.

2.   Thread the chicken kebabs on skewers and grill in a preheated grill for about 10 minutes or until the chicken is cooked.

3.   To make the dip: Add all the ingredients of the dip to a blender. Blend until smooth. Transfer into a bowl.

4.   Garnish the kebabs with shredded cabbage, onion rings and lemon wedges. Serve the kebabs with the dip.

Cauliflower "Mashed potatoes"

Serves: 4-5

Ingredients:

- 2 medium heads of cauliflower or 1 large head cauliflower, cut into florets
- 6 cloves garlic
- 1/4 cup fresh dill, chopped + extra for garnishing
- Sea salt to taste
- Pepper powder to taste
- 1 tablespoon butter
- 2 tablespoons coconut milk

Instructions:

1.   Steam the broccoli, cauliflower and garlic until very soft.
2.   Transfer into a bowl
3.   Add coconut milk, dill, butter, salt and pepper. Puree with an immersion blender.
4.   Garnish with dill and serve.

Beef Coconut Curry

Serves: 4

Ingredients:

1 large onion, chopped

1 1/2 pounds grass-fed beef

6 cloves finely chopped garlic,

1 green chopped bell pepper

1 red chopped bell pepper

2 teaspoons salt or to taste

Pepper powder to taste

2 tablespoons coconut oil

3/4 cup tomato paste

1 inch finely grated fresh ginger

2 teaspoons ground turmeric

2 tablespoons curry powder

1 1/2 teaspoons ground cumin

1 1/2 teaspoons ground coriander

1 teaspoon cayenne pepper or to taste

2 cans full fat coconut milk

1 sliced head cabbage

2 tablespoons lemon juice

Instructions:

1.　　Mix together, turmeric, cumin, cayenne pepper, salt, pepper, curry powder and coriander in a bowl and set aside.

2.　　Place a large skillet over medium high heat. Add oil. When oil melts, add onions, bell peppers and garlic and sauté for a couple of minutes.

3.　　Add beef and cook breaking it simultaneously. Cook until beef is brown.

4.　　Lower heat. Add tomato paste and ginger and stir. Add spice powder mixture and mix well.

5.　　Remove from heat. Add coconut milk and lime juice and mix well. Keep warm.

6.　　To steam cabbage: Place a saucepan filled with water over medium heat. Bring to a boil. Add cabbage and cook until tender.

7.　　Strain and place on individual serving plates. Serve coconut beef curry over it and serve immediately.

Chapter 10: Desserts Recipes

Frozen Yogurt Popsicles

Serves: 12

Ingredients:

- 1 cup heavy whipping cream
- 2 cups low fat Greek yogurt
- 2 teaspoons vanilla
- 1 pound frozen strawberries
- 1 pound frozen mangoes

Instructions:

1.   Remove the strawberries and mango about 15 minutes before preparing.

2.   Add all the ingredients to the blender and blend until smooth.

3.   Serve immediately if you prefer soft serve else freeze in an ice cream maker according to the instruction of the manufacturer and serve.

Chocolate Squares

Serves: 10-12

Ingredients:

- 2 teaspoons coffee powder
- 4 ounces of creamy peanut butter / almond butter / hazelnut butter
- A pinch salt
- 1/2 cup peanuts / almonds / hazelnuts, roasted, chopped
- 6 tablespoons butter
- 6 ounces 70 % dark chocolate
- 1 teaspoon vanilla

Instructions:

1. Add butter and chocolate to a microwave safe bowl and microwave until chocolate melts.
2. Add rest of the ingredients except peanuts.
3. Transfer on to a greased and lined baking sheet. Sprinkle the nuts of your choice and let it chill.
4. Chop into 1 inch squares and serve.

Steamed Cinnamon Coconut Milk Egg Custard

Serves: 8-10

Ingredients:

- ½ teaspoon ground cinnamon
- 1/2 tsp salt
- 4 eggs
- 4 egg yolks
- 2/3 cup granulated sweetener like Splenda
- 4 cups unsweetened coconut milk

Instructions:

1.   Whisk together eggs and egg yolks in a bowl. Add sweetener and mix well.

2.   To another bowl add salt, coconut milk and cinnamon. Whisk well.

3.   Pour the coconut milk mixture into the egg yolk mixture. Whisk well.

4.   Pour into greased ramekins.

5.   Place a baking tray with water in it in a preheated oven. Place the ramekins into a baking tray that is filled

with water.

6.   Bake in a preheated oven at 300° F for about 30 minutes or until the custard is set.

7.   Serve either warm or cold.

Pineapple Coconut Granita

Serves: 8

Ingredients:

- 1 cup sucralose sweetener (sugar substitute)
- 1 1/2 teaspoons coconut extract
- 1 whole peeled, chopped pineapple
- 1 cup water

Instructions:

1. Add pineapple into a blender and blend until smooth.

2. Place a saucepan over high heat. Add sugar substitute and water and simmer until sugar substitute dissolves. Remove from heat. Cool slightly.

3. Add to the blender along with the pineapple and blend until smooth.

4. Transfer into a freezer safe container. Add coconut extract and stir well.

5. Place in the freezer. Remove from the freezer every 30 minutes and break the mixture with a fork. Place it

each time in the freezer. Continue doing this until the mixture is in tiny pieces and frozen as well.

6.   When done, cover and freeze until use.

Chocolate Peppermint Cupcakes

Serves: 12-15

Ingredients:

- 4 tablespoons unsweetened cocoa powder
- 1/2 teaspoon salt
- 2 servings crushed peppermint sugar free candy
- 1/4 teaspoon peppermint extract
- A pinch of stevia (optional)
- Food coloring of your choice (optional)
- 1/2 cup unsweetened coconut milk
- 6 large eggs
- 8 ounces of cream cheese
- 14 tablespoons unsalted butter
- 2 teaspoons vanilla extract
- 1/2 cup xylitol
- 12 tablespoons powdered erythritol
- 8 tablespoons coconut flour
- 1/2 teaspoon baking powder

Instructions:

1.   Mix together all the dry ingredients in a bowl.

2.   Whisk together peppermint extract, 6 tablespoons melted butter, eggs, coconut milk, erythritol and vanilla.

3.   Add the dry ingredients to it and whisk until well combined.

4.   Pour into lined muffin tins (Fill up to 3/4). Line with paper cups.

7.   Bake in a preheated oven at 375° F   for about 15 minutes or until a toothpick when inserted comes out clean.

5.   Remove from the oven. Place on wire racks to cool.

6.   Meanwhile make the frosting as follows: Add cream cheese to a bowl and beat until smooth with an electric mixer.

7.   Add the remaining erythritol and beat for a minute. Add stevia and food coloring if using.

8.   Spread the frosting on top of the cupcakes. Sprinkle peppermint candies and serve.

Flan

Serves: 8

Ingredients:

- 10 packets sugar substitute or to taste
- 1/2 teaspoon ground cinnamon
- 2 cups heavy cream
- 10 eggs
- 2 cups water
- 2 teaspoons almond extract

Instructions:

1.   Add all the ingredients except cinnamon to a blender and blend until smooth.

2.   Pour into individual ramekins. Sprinkle cinnamon on top. Place a baking tray with water in it in a preheated oven. Place the ramekins into a baking tray that is filled with water.

3.   Bake in a preheated oven at 300° F for about 30 minutes or until the flan is set.

4.   Serve either warm or cold.

Pineapple Mango Layer Cake

Serves: 16-20

Ingredients:

- 1/2 cup melted and cooled unsalted butter,
- 1 cup heavy cream
- 1 pineapple, peeled, cored, thinly slice half the pineapple and chop the other half into small pieces
- 1 mango, thinly slice half the mango and chop the other half into small pieces
- 2 cups soy flour
- 2 teaspoons baking powder
- 1/2 teaspoon salt
- 12 large separated eggs,
- 26 tablespoons granular sugar substitute (sucralose), divided
- 4 teaspoons almond extract

Instructions:

1.   To make the cake: Mix together soy flour, baking powder and salt in a bowl.

2.   Whisk the whites using an electric mixer (keep the speed medium) for a couple of minutes.

3.   Add 24 tablespoons of the sugar substitute slowly, beating simultaneously until stiff peaks are formed.

4.   To another bowl add yolks, almond extract and butter. Whisk well.

5.   With the mixer running, gently pour the yolk mixture into the white mixture. Whisk until well combined. Stop the electric mixer now.

6.   Gently fold the flour mixture into the egg mixture.

7.   Divide the batter amongst 2 greased baking dishes.

8.   Bake in a preheated oven at 350 degrees F for about 30 minutes or until a toothpick when inserted comes out clean.

9.   Remove from the oven and keep aside to cool for a while. Transfer on to a wire rack to cool completely.

10.   To arrange the cake: Add cream and 2 tablespoons sugar substitute to a bowl and whisk well with an electric mixer until soft peaks are formed.

11.   Place one of the cakes on a plate. Spoon half the

whipped cream over it. Spread it all over the cake.

12.   Scatter the mango and pineapple pieces all over the cake.

13.   Place the other cake over the mango and pineapple layer. Spread the remaining whipped cream all over the top of the cake.

14.   Decorate with sliced mangoes and pineapple.

15.   Slice and serve.

Chilled Lemon Cheesecake

Serves: 12-15

Ingredients:

- Zest of 2 lemons or to taste
- A large pinch of salt
- Thinly sliced lemon for garnishing
- 1 teaspoon shredded lemon zest
- 2 ounces of gelatin powder
- 2 cups water
- 2 pounds of cream cheese
- 12 sachets sugar substitute or to taste
- Juice of 2 lemons

Instructions:

1. Add water to a saucepan. Sprinkle gelatin powder all over the water. Keep it aside for about 10 minutes to dissolve.

2. Meanwhile add cream cheese and sugar substitute to a bowl. Beat until creamy.

3. Place the saucepan with gelatin over low heat. Stir

constantly until the gelatin dissolves. Remove from heat.

4.   Pour the gelatin mixture into the cream cheese mixture and beat well.

5.   Add salt, lemon juice, lemon zest and blend again.

6.   Transfer the beaten mixture into a cake tin. Refrigerate overnight.

7.   Garnish with lemon slices and shredded lemon zest.

Fruit Salad

Serves: 8

Ingredients:

- 4 peaches, diced
- 1 ounce of triple sec
- Juice of 2 lemons
- Juice of 2 oranges
- 1/4 cup mint leaves, for garnish
- 2 peeled, seeded, diced mangoes
- 4 pints sliced in half strawberries
- 2 pints of blueberries
- 5 sliced, peeled kiwis
- 2 pints of raspberries

Instructions:

1.   Add all the ingredients to a large bowl. Toss well. Refrigerate and serve chilled garnished with mint leaves.

Decadent Chocolate Ice Cream

Serves: 12-15

Ingredients:

- 6 cups heavy cream
- 1 1/2 cups erythritol or sucralose based sweetener
- 1/2 teaspoon salt
- 8 large egg
- 4 egg yolks
- 1 1/2 cups unsweetened cocoa
- 1 teaspoon pure almond extract
- 4 teaspoons vanilla extract

Instructions:

1.   Place a heavy bottomed pan over medium heat. Add cream and let it heat for a while. Remove from heat.

2.   Whisk together with an electric mixer, sugar substitute, salt, eggs, yolks and cocoa until thick and smooth.

3.   Add about a cup of the heated cream and gently whisk. Pour this mixture into the pan of cream whisking simultaneously.

4.   Place the pan over medium heat and continue whisking until it thickens slightly. Do not heat beyond 170° F.

5.   Remove from heat and transfer into a bowl. Add vanilla and almond extract and whisk again.

6.   Refrigerate for at least 2-3 hours. Add the chilled mixture into the ice cream maker and use according to the instructions of the manufacturers.

7.   If you prefer soft serve, serve immediately else freeze for 3-4 hours and serve.

Chapter 11: Smoothies

Chocolate Smoothie

Serves: 2

Ingredients:

- 6 tablespoons half and half
- 1 cup water
- Ice cubes as required
- Sugar free chocolate syrup (optional)
- 2 tablespoons unsweetened cocoa
- 2 scoops chocolate whey protein
- 1 1/2 tablespoons decaffeinated instant coffee powder

Instructions:

1.   Add all the ingredients into the blender and blend until smooth. Add more water to dilute the smoothie if you desire a smoothie of thinner consistency.

2.   Pour into tall glasses. Drizzle sugar free chocolate syrup if using and serve.

Chocolate Peanut Butter Smoothie

Serves: 2

Ingredients:

- 2 cups coconut milk
- 1/8 teaspoon stevia
- 1/2 teaspoon ground cinnamon
- 1/8 teaspoon salt
- 2 scoops chocolate whey protein
- 4 tablespoons natural creamy peanut butter

Instructions:

1.	Add all the ingredients into the blender and blend until smooth. Add more milk to dilute the smoothie if you desire a smoothie of thinner consistency.
2.	Pour into tall glasses and serve with crushed ice.

Pineapple Almond Milk Smoothie

Serves: 2

Ingredients:

- 1 cup low fat Greek yogurt
- 1 cup unsweetened almond milk
- 4 sachets sweetener of your choice or to taste
- 40 blanched whole almonds
- Ice cubes as required
- 5 ounces diced, frozen fresh pineapple

Instructions:

1.   To blanch almonds: Place the almonds in a small saucepan filled with water. Bring to a boil. Simmer for a minute. Drain and rinse with cold water. Remove the skin.

2.   Blend together all the ingredients until smooth. Retain a couple of almonds for garnishing.

3.   Serve in tall glasses garnished with slivered almonds.

Blackberry Smoothie

Serves: 2

Ingredients:

- 1 teaspoon vanilla extract
- 2 tablespoons ground golden flaxseed meal
- 1/4 teaspoon ground allspice
- 2 scoops vanilla whey protein
- 1/2 cup frozen blackberries
- 2 cups unsweetened vanilla almond milk or coconut milk

Instructions:

1.   Add all the ingredients into the blender and blend until smooth. Add more milk to dilute the smoothie if you desire a smoothie of thinner consistency.
2.   Pour into tall glasses and serve with crushed ice.

Kiwi Strawberry Smoothie

Serves: 3

Ingredients:

- 1 peeled, chopped kiwi
- 2 teaspoons orange zest
- 1 teaspoon vanilla extract
- Ice cubes
- 1 cup almond milk or skimmed
- 1 cup low fat plain Greek yogurt
- 1 cup strawberries, chopped

Instructions:

1.   Add all the ingredients to a blender and blend until smooth.
2.   Pour into tall glasses and serve immediately.

Peanut butter Smoothie

Serves: 2

Ingredients:

- 4 cups strawberries, fresh or frozen, chopped
- 1 frozen chopped banana
- Ice as required
- 2 tablespoons smooth peanut butter
- 8 ounces plain nonfat Greek yogurt

Instructions:

1.   Add all the ingredients to the blender and blend until smooth. Add yogurt or water to dilute the smoothie if you desire a smoothie of thinner consistency.
2.   Pour into tall glasses and serve.

Mango and Banana Overnight Oats Smoothie

Serves: 2

Ingredients:

For the oats:

- 1/3 cup oats
- 1/2 tablespoon ground flaxseed
- 1 small ripe banana
- 3/4 cup almond milk
- 2 tablespoons chia seeds
- Sweetener of your choice

For the smoothie:
- 1 ripe peeled, sliced banana
- 1/2 mango, chopped into chunks
- 1 tablespoon ground flaxseed
- 1 cup almond milk

Instructions:

1.   Add ingredients of the smoothie into your blender. Blend until smooth.

2.   Pour into tall glasses.

3.   To make the oats layer: Peel and chop the banana. Add it to the blender along with almond milk, sweetener, and ground flaxseed. Blend until smooth.

4.   Add oats and chia seeds. Stir well and pour it over the pureed mango and banana.

5.   Chill in the refrigerator overnight and serve.

Detox Green Smoothie

Serves: 2

Ingredients:

- 1/2 cup mint
- 6 chopped stalks celery
- 2-inch piece peeled chopped fresh ginger
- 2 tablespoons lemon juice
- 1/2 cup water
- 2 chopped short cucumber
- 1 cup torn lettuce leaves
- 2 cups torn spinach
- 1 cup parsley

Instructions:

1.   Add all the ingredients into the blender and blend until smooth. Add more water to dilute the smoothie if you desire a smoothie of thinner consistency.
2.   Pour into tall glasses and serve with crushed ice.

Cucumber Cooler

Serves: 2

Ingredients:

- 2/3 cup water
- 1/2 cup cold water
- Ice cubes as required
- 2 cups peeled, deseeded, chopped cucumber,
- 1/2 cup fresh mint leaves + extra to garnish

Instructions:

1.   Add all the ingredients to the blender and blend until smooth.
2.   Pour into tall glasses and serve garnished with a mint leaf.

Spinach Smoothie

Serves: 3

Ingredients:

- 3 cups vanilla almond milk
- 1 teaspoon vanilla extract
- 2 scoops vanilla whey protein
- 2 cups spinach, torn

Instructions:

1.   Add all the ingredients into the blender and blend until smooth. Add more milk to dilute the smoothie if you desire a smoothie of thinner consistency.
2.   Pour into tall glasses and serve with crushed ice.

Fat burning Green Tea Smoothie

Serves: 2

Ingredients:

- 1 cup pineapple pieces
- 1 1/2 cups caffeinated green tea or more according to the consistency you desire
- 1 cup broccoli florets
- 1/2 cup cauliflower florets

Instructions:

1.   Add all the ingredients to the blender and blend until smooth.
2.   Pour into tall glasses and serve with crushed ice.

Tropical Fruits Smoothie

Serves: 4

Ingredients:

- 1/2 cup ripe papaya chunks
- 2 tablespoons flax seeds
- 2 tablespoons cashew nuts
- Ice cubes
- 3 cups almond milk
- 1 small peeled, chopped banana
- 1/2 cup ripe peeled, chopped into chunks mango
- 1/2 cup frozen pineapple chunks
- 1/2 peeled, seeded, chopped into segments orange

Instructions:

1. Add all the ingredients to a blender and blend until smooth.
2. Pour into tall glasses and serve immediately.

Breakfast Green Smoothie

Serves: 4

Ingredients:

- 2 cups frozen mango
- 1 1/2 cups plain nonfat yogurt
- 1 teaspoon vanilla
- Ice cubes as required
- 1 medium peeled, chopped banana
- 4 cups baby spinach, packed
- 2 cups soy milk
- 1/2 cup whole oats

Instructions:

1.   Add milk, yogurt, and oats to the blender and blend for about 12-15 seconds.

2.   Add rest of the ingredients and blend until smooth.

3.   Pour into tall glasses and serve immediately.

Coconut-Vanilla Shake

Serves: 3

Ingredients:

- 2 cans (14 ounces each) coconut cream
- 1 teaspoon vanilla extract
- 4 scoops vanilla whey protein

Instructions:

1.   Add all the ingredients into the blender and blend until smooth. Add more water to dilute the smoothie if you desire a smoothie of thinner consistency.

2.   Pour into tall glasses and serve with crushed ice.

Breakfast Chocolate Smoothie

Serves: 4

Ingredients:

- 4 tablespoons unsweetened cocoa powder
- 3 individual packets Splenda or any natural sweetener to taste
- Ice cubes as required
- 3 cups vanilla soy milk
- 3/4 pitted, peeled, chopped avocado
- 1 1/2 medium peeled, chopped banana

Instructions:

1. Add all the ingredients to a blender and blend until smooth.
2. Pour into tall glasses and serve immediately.

Dairy free latte

Serves: 3

Ingredients:

- 1/4 teaspoon ground cloves
- 1/4 teaspoon ground cinnamon
- 2 tablespoons cocoa / instant coffee powder
- 4 eggs
- 3 cups hot water
- 4 tablespoons coconut oil
- 1/4 teaspoon vanilla extract
- 1/2 teaspoon ground ginger

Instructions:

1.   Add all the ingredients into the blender and blend until smooth.
2.   Pour into tall glasses and serve with crushed ice.

Strawberry Shake

Serves: 2

Ingredients:

- 2 teaspoons bee pollen
- 15 -20 frozen strawberries
- 2 glasses of water
- 2 scoops whey protein powder

Instructions:

1.   Blend together all the ingredients until smooth. Transfer into tall glasses.
2.   Serve with crushed ice.

Chapter 12: Salad Recipes

Green Salad

Serves: 4

Ingredients:

For green salad:
- 1 pound Brussels sprouts, shredded
- ½ pound mustard greens, torn
- 2 green apples, cored, halved, thinly sliced
- Juice of ½ lemon
- Cooked chicken pieces (optional)

For vinaigrette:
- 6-8 tablespoons olive oil or extra virgin olive oil
- ¼ teaspoon salt
- 2 tablespoons lemon juice or vinegar
- ¼ teaspoon pepper
- 1 clove garlic, minced
- 1 tablespoon fresh herbs, minced
- ½ teaspoon honey or to taste (optional)

Instructions:

1.   To make vinaigrette: Add all the ingredients of the vinaigrette into a small bottle. Fasten with a lid. Shake vigorously until well combined. Refrigerate until use.

2.   Add Brussels sprouts and mustard greens into an airtight container and refrigerate until use. Please make sure that the Brussels sprouts and greens are well dried (after rinsing) before packing it into the refrigerator.

3.   Sprinkle lemon juice over the apples and toss well. Cover and refrigerator until use.

4.   To serve: Add chicken and apples to the greens and toss.

5.   Pour as much dressing as required and toss well.

6.   Serve immediately.

Upside-Down BBQ Chicken Bowl

Serves: 6

Ingredients:

- 15-18 ounces of broccoli slaw, shredded
- 1 ½ tablespoons olive oil
- 1 large red bell pepper, deseeded, chopped
- 2-2 ½ cups fresh or frozen corn kernels
- 3 cups kale, discard hard stems and leaves, finely shredded
- 1/3 cup ranch dressing
- ¾ cup almonds, sliced
- Salt and freshly ground pepper to taste

To serve:

- 3 cups BBQ chicken, shredded
- 6 garlic bread slices

Instructions:

1.   Add broccoli slaw into a large bowl. Drizzle ranch dressing on it.

2.   Place a skillet over high heat. Add oil and heat. Add corn and bell pepper and sauté until brown. Add kale and sauté until the kale wilts. Cool for a while.

3.   Transfer into the bowl of broccoli slaw. Add salt and pepper and toss well.

4.   Toss well and place in an airtight container. Refrigerate until use. It can last for 3 days.

5.   To serve: Add almonds and toss well.

6.   Divide the salad among 6 bowls. Divide the BBQ chicken over the salad.

7.   Place a slice of garlic bread on each and serve.

Garlicky Chickpea and Fennel Salad with Baked Goat Cheese

Serves: 6

Ingredients:

- 18 ounces of fresh goat's cheese
- 1 ½ cans (15 ounces each) garbanzo beans, drained, rinsed, pat dried
- 1 ½ cups bread crumbs
- 3 tablespoons olive oil
- 2-2 ½ teaspoons kosher salt, divided
- 6 large egg whites
- 6 medium fennel bulbs, thinly sliced
- ½ cup fresh parsley, chopped
- 1/3 cup fennel fronds
- ¾ cup tahini roasted garlic dressing
- ¾ teaspoon red pepper flakes or to taste
- Freshly ground black pepper to taste
- Juice of 1 ½ lemons

Instructions:

1.   Form 1-inch ball of the goat's cheese. Flatten it thick rounds.   Store in the refrigerator in an airtight container until use.

2.   Place a large skillet with oil over medium high heat. Add garbanzo beans in a single layer. Do not stir for a while until the underside is light brown. Sprinkle salt and red pepper flakes and stir. Cook until golden brown.

3.   Cool and transfer into an airtight container. Refrigerate until use.

4.   Mix together in a bowl, breadcrumbs, salt and red pepper flakes.

5.   Sprinkle lemon juice over fennel and refrigerate until use.

6.   To serve: Dip each of the goat cheese discs into the whites and then dredge into the breadcrumb mixture and place on a lined baking sheet.

7.   Bake in a preheated oven at 375°F until golden brown.

8.   Mix together rest of the ingredients into a bowl and toss.

9.   Divide into 6 plates. Top with cheese discs and serve.

Apple Pecan and Feta Salad with Honey Apple Dressing

Serves: 4

Ingredients:

For salad:

- 12 cups kale, discard hard stems and ribs, torn
- 1/2 cup cranberries
- 12 tablespoons feta cheese, crumbled
- 8 apples, cored, halved, thinly sliced
- 8 tablespoons pecans

For honey apple vinaigrette:

- 8 tablespoons honey
- 8 tablespoons olive oil
- Salt and pepper to taste
- 4 tablespoons apple cider vinegar

Instructions:

1.   Add all the ingredients of the dressing into a small jar. Fasten with a lid. Shake vigorously until it is well combined. Refrigerate until use.

2.   Add all the ingredients of the salad into an airtight container and refrigerate until use.

3.   To serve: Pour as much dressing as required and toss well. Serve immediately.

4.   The salad can last for 3 days.

Strawberry Poppy Seed and Bacon Salad

Serves: 8

Ingredients:

- 8 cups romaine lettuce, chopped
- 16 strips bacon, cooked, crumbled
- 2 cups feta cheese, crumbled
- 4 cups strawberries, chopped
- 1 red onion, chopped

For dressing:

- 2 teaspoons garlic, minced
- 2/3 cup sugar
- ½ cup strawberries, chopped
- ½ teaspoon salt
- 2 teaspoons red onion, chopped
- 2/3 cup white vinegar
- 1 cup olive oil
- 2 tablespoons poppy seeds

Instructions:

1.   Mix together all the salad ingredients except feta cheese in a bowl.

2.   Cover and chill in the refrigerator until use.

3.   Add all the ingredients of the dressing into a blender and blend until smooth.

4.   Transfer into a bowl. Cover and refrigerate until use.

5.   To serve: Pour dressing over the salad and toss well.

6.   Sprinkle feta cheese and serve.

Fresh and Springy Walnut, Radish and Apple Salad

Serves: 4

Ingredients:

For salad:

- 1 1/2 cup walnuts
- 12 cups mixed greens
- 10 radishes, thinly sliced
- 4 stalk celery, chopped
- 1 green apple, cored, thinly sliced

For the dressing:

- 12 tablespoons raw almond butter
- 1/2 teaspoon salt or to taste
- 8 teaspoons sesame oil, toasted
- 4 tablespoons unseasoned rice wine vinegar
- 4 tablespoons maple syrup

Instructions:

1.   Soak apple slices in a bowl of salted water for a while. Drain and pat dry.

2.   Add all the ingredients of the dressing into a small jar. Fasten with a lid. Shake vigorously until it is well combined. Refrigerate until use.

3.   Add all the ingredients of the salad into an airtight container and refrigerate until use.

4.   To serve: Pour as much dressing as required and toss well. If the dressing is very thick, add some water and stir.

5.   Serve immediately.

6.   The salad can last for 3 days.

Chapter 13: Soup Recipes

Chicken Noodle Soup

Serves: 8

Ingredients:
- 8 cups chicken stock
- 3 tablespoons butter or coconut oil
- 3 medium stalks celery, sliced
- 1 large onion, chopped
- 3 medium carrots, chopped sliced or chopped
- 8 ounces of gluten free noodles or egg noodles
- 1 ½ cups chicken breast, chopped into small pieces, cooked
- Salt and pepper to taste
- 1 ½ tablespoons all-purpose seasoning
- 4 cloves garlic, minced
- ¼ teaspoon cayenne powder
- 1 ½ tablespoons tapioca flour mixed with 2 tablespoons water

Instructions:

1.   Place a large soup pot over medium heat. Add butter. When butter melts, add onions, carrots and celery. Sauté until onions are translucent.

2.   Add garlic, salt and pepper and sauté until garlic is fragrant.

3.   Add rest of the ingredients except tapioca mixture and cook until noodles are al dente. Add tapioca mixture and stir constantly until thick.

4.   Simmer for another 5 minutes.

5.   Cool and pour into mason jars. Fasten the lids. Refrigerate until use. Alternately pour into freezer safe pouches and freeze.

6.   Heat thoroughly and serve.

Tomato Soup

Serves: 8

Ingredients:

- 8 cups chicken stock or vegetable stock
- 6-8 tablespoons butter or coconut oil
- 1 large onion, chopped
- 8 cloves garlic, chopped
- 6 medium carrots, chopped
- 4 tablespoons tomato paste
- 10 large tomatoes, deseeded, juices scooped out
- 4 teaspoons raw honey
- Salt and pepper to taste
- ¼ cup fresh basil or 2 tablespoons dried basil

Instructions:

1. Place a large soup pot over medium heat. Add butter. When butter melts, add onions and carrots. Sauté until onions are translucent.

2. Add garlic, tomato paste, salt and pepper. Sauté for a minute.

3. Add rest of the ingredients except honey and bring

to the boil. Lower heat and simmer until tender.

4.   Blend until smooth adding honey while blending.

5.   Cool and pour into mason jars. Fasten the lids. Refrigerate until use. Alternately pour into freezer safe pouches and freeze.

6.   Heat thoroughly and serve.

Kid Friendly Creamy Vegetable Soup

Serves: 8

Ingredients:

- 2 ½ pounds mixed chopped vegetables
- 3 cups potatoes, cubed
- 4 cloves garlic, chopped
- 3 cups onions, chopped
- 8 cups water
- Salt and pepper to taste
- 2 tablespoons butter or coconut oil

Instructions:

1.   Place a large soup pot over medium heat. Add butter. When butter melts, add onions. Sauté until onions are translucent.

2.   Add garlic, salt and pepper. Sauté for a minute.

3.   Add rest of the ingredients and bring to the boil. Lower heat and simmer until tender.

4.   Blend until smooth.

5.   Cool and pour into mason jars. Fasten the lids. Refrigerate until use. Alternately pour into freezer safe pouches and freeze.

6.   Heat thoroughly and serve.

Tomato-Seashell Soup

Serves: 4

Ingredients:

- 2 cups low sodium marinara sauce
- 2 cups cooked whole grain small shell pasta
- Salt and pepper to taste
- 2 cups fresh spinach, chopped
- 2 cups zucchini noodles or chopped zucchini
- 6 tablespoons parmesan cheese, finely grated

Instructions:

1. Divide marinara between 4 wide jars of 1 pint each.
2. Layer with the remaining ingredients in any manner you desire.
3. Fasten the lids and refrigerate until use.
4. To serve: Pour very hot water into the jars leaving about an inch from the top.
5. Cover with lid and let it sit for 2 minutes before serving.

Miso Noodle Soup

Serves: 4

Ingredients:

- 4 tablespoons white miso mixed with 2 tablespoons warm water
- 4 teaspoons sesame oil, toasted
- 1 1/2 cup red cabbage, thinly sliced
- 8 shiitake mushroom caps, thinly sliced
- 16 thin slices jalapeño
- 2 large hardboiled eggs, chopped
- 2 cloves garlic, grated
- 2 cups cooked flat brown rice (or 4 ounces uncooked pad Thai noodles)
- 2 green onions, thinly sliced
- 4 tablespoons fresh cilantro, chopped

Instructions:

1.   Mix together oil, miso mixture and garlic in a bowl and divide between 2 wide jars of 1 pint each.
2.   Layer with the remaining ingredients in any

manner you desire.

3.	Fasten the lids and refrigerate until use.

4.	To serve: Pour very hot water into the jars leaving about an inch from the top. Cover with lid and let it sit for 2 minutes before serving.

Chickpeas and Sausage Pesto Soup

Serves: 2

Ingredients:

- 1 cup canned chickpeas, rinsed, drained
- 4 tablespoons refrigerated prepared pesto
- 2/3 cup Swiss chard, discard hard stems and ribs, thinly sliced
- 1 medium carrot, cut into matchsticks
- 4 ounces cooked sundried tomato chicken sausages, diced
- 6 grape tomatoes, quartered

Instructions:

1. Divide chickpeas between 2 wide jars of 1 pint each.
2. Layer with the remaining ingredients in any manner you desire.
3. Fasten the lids and refrigerate until use.
4. To serve: Pour very hot water into the jars leaving about an inch from the top.
5. Cover with lid and let it sit for 2 minutes before serving.

Chapter 14: Side Dishes Recipes

Herbed Quinoa

Serves: 8

Ingredients:

For quinoa:

- 5 ½ cups low sodium chicken or vegetable broth
- 3 cups quinoa
- ½ cup fresh lemon juice

For herb dressing:

- ½ cup extra virgin olive oil
- 1 ½ cups fresh basil leaves, chopped
- 2 tablespoons fresh thyme leaves, chopped
- ½ cup fresh parsley leaves, chopped
- 4 teaspoons lemon zest, grated
- Freshly ground pepper and salt to taste

Instructions:

1.   Place a saucepan over medium high heat with all the ingredients of quinoa in it. Bring to the boil.

2.   Lower heat and cover with a lid. Simmer until all the broth is absorbed. When done, fluff with a fork.

3.   Mix together all the ingredients of the dressing and pour over the quinoa. Toss well. Transfer into an airtight container.

4.   Refrigerate until use.

5.   Heat before serving.

Orange Glazed Carrots

Serves: 8

Ingredients:

- 2 pounds of carrots, cut into 1 inch chunks
- 2 tablespoons unsalted butter
- 2 tablespoons fresh dill, chopped
- 2 cups fresh orange juice
- Freshly ground pepper and salt to taste

Instructions:

1. Add carrots and orange juice into a large saucepan. Place the saucepan over medium heat. Pour water to cover the carrots. Add salt, pepper and butter and bring to the boil.

2. Lower heat and simmer until tender and the liquid almost dried up. The carrots will have a glazed look.

3. Cool and store in an airtight container. Refrigerate until use.

4. To serve: Heat in a microwave and serve garnished with dill.

Easy Garlic Parmesan Knots

Serves: 8

Ingredients:

- 2 tablespoons unsalted butter, melted
- ½ teaspoon garlic powder
- ¼ teaspoon dried parsley flakes
- ¼ teaspoon dried oregano
- 8 ounces tube refrigerated buttermilk biscuits (4 biscuits)
- 1 tablespoon parmesan cheese, freshly grated
- 1/8 teaspoon salt

Instructions:

1.   Mix together in a bowl all the ingredients except buttermilk biscuits. Set aside.

2.   Grease a baking sheet with oil and set aside.

3.   Cut each biscuit into 2 halves. Take one piece and roll until about 5 inches long and about ½ inch thick. It will look like a rope.

4.   Tie a knot with the roll and tuck the ends. Place on

the greased baking sheet. Repeat with the remaining 7 pieces.

5.   Brush the butter mixture over the knots.

6.   Bake in a preheated oven at 400°F until golden brown.

7.   Brush with some more of the butter mixture and serve.

8.   To store: Store in an airtight container. Warm in an oven. Brush with butter mixture and serve.

Baked Parmesan Mushrooms

Serves: 8

Ingredients:

- 3 pounds Cremini mushrooms, thinly sliced
- ½ cup fresh lemon juice
- 4 teaspoons dried thyme
- Salt and freshly ground pepper to taste
- 6 tablespoons olive oil
- Zest of 2 lemons, grated
- ½ cup parmesan, grated
- 6 tablespoons olive oil

Instructions:

1.	Grease a baking sheet with oil and spread the mushrooms all over the sheet.

2.	Drizzle oil lemon juice on it. Sprinkle rest of the ingredients on it and toss lightly. Spread it all over the sheet.

3.	Refrigerate until use.

4.	To serve: Bake in a preheated oven at 375°F for 12-15 minutes or until brown. Shake the mushrooms half way through baking.

5.	Serve immediately.

Jalapeño Cornbread Muffins

Serves: 24

Ingredients:

- 2 cups yellow cornmeal
- 2 cups all-purpose flour
- 1 teaspoon salt
- 1 cup unsalted butter, melted
- 4 large eggs
- 4 jalapeños, deseeded, diced
- 1 teaspoon baking soda
- 2 cups buttermilk
- 1 cup sugar
- 2 tablespoons honey
- ½ cup cheddar cheese, shredded

Instructions:

1. Mix together in a large bowl all the dry ingredients.
2. Mix together in another bowl all the wet ingredients and sugar. Pour this mixture into the bowl of dry ingredients and mix well into a batter.

3.   Add jalapeños and cheese and fold lightly. Spoon the batter into greased muffin tins. Fill up to ¾.

4.   Bake in a preheated oven at 375°F for 15-17 minutes or until a toothpick when inserted in the center comes out clean.

5.   When done, cool completely.

6.   Store in an airtight container in the refrigerator.

7.   Use as required.

Parmesan Crusted Scalloped Potatoes

Serves: 8

Ingredients:

- 3 cups heavy cream
- 2 sprigs fresh thyme
- 4 pounds of russet potatoes, peeled, cut into 1/8-inch-thick slices
- 1 ¼ cups parmesan cheese, freshly grated + extra to serve
- 4 cloves garlic, pressed
- 1/8 teaspoon nutmeg, grated
- Freshly ground pepper and salt to taste

Instructions:

1.   Grease 2 pie plates or baking dish with oil and set aside.

2.   Place a saucepan over medium heat. Add cream, garlic, thyme and nutmeg and heat for 2-3 minutes. Stir all the while.

3.   Place a layer of potatoes in each of the prepared

dish. The potato slices can be overlapped. Sprinkle salt and pepper.

4.   Pour 1/3 the cream mixture over it.

5.   Sprinkle 1/3 the Parmesan cheese over it.

6.   Repeat the above 2 steps twice.

7.   Bake in a preheated oven at 375°F for 35-40 minutes or until the potatoes are tender. Cover with cling wrap.

8.   Cool and refrigerate until use. It can last for 2-3 days.

9.   To serve: Sprinkle extra Parmesan cheese on it.

10.   Bake for 10 minutes and then broil until golden brown.

11.   Serve immediately.

Chapter 15: Snack Recipes

Baked Parmesan Zucchini

Serves: 8

Ingredients:

- 8 zucchinis, quartered lengthwise
- 1 teaspoon dried thyme
- 1 teaspoon dried basil
- Freshly ground pepper to taste
- 1 teaspoon dried thyme
- ½ teaspoon garlic powder
- 4 tablespoons olive oil
- Salt to taste
- ¼ cup fresh parsley leaves, chopped

Instructions:

1.   Grease a baking sheet with a little oil and set aside.

2.   Mix together in a bowl, Parmesan, dried herbs, garlic powder, salt and pepper.

3.   Place zucchini on the prepared baking sheet. Bake

in batches if required.

4.   Drizzle oil over the zucchini pieces.

5.   Sprinkle the cheese mixture on it.

6.   Bake in a preheated oven at 350°F for 15 minutes or until tender. Transfer into a container. Cover and set-aside until use.

7.   To serve: Broil for a few minutes in an oven until crisp.

8.   Sprinkle parsley and serve.

Baked Asparagus Fries

Serves: 12

Ingredients:

- 2 cups panko bread crumbs
- Freshly ground black pepper to taste
- ½ cup all-purpose flour
- 1 cup parmesan cheese, grated
- Salt to taste
- 2 pounds of asparagus, trimmed
- 4 large eggs, beaten

Instructions:

1.   Grease a baking sheet with a little oil and set aside.
2.   Add panko breadcrumbs, Parmesan, salt and pepper into a large bowl.
3.   Place flour on a plate.
4.   First roll the asparagus in the flour. Next dip it in the bowl of beaten eggs and finally roll in the bowl of panko breadcrumbs. Press lightly so that the breadcrumbs are well coated.

5.   Place the asparagus on the baking sheet. Do not overlap.

6.   Bake in a preheated oven at 350°F for 15 minutes or until crisp.

7.   Cool and store in an airtight container until use.

Potato Chips

Serves: 4-6

Ingredients:

- 4 large potatoes, rinsed, sliced into 1/8 inch thin slices using a slicer
- Freshly ground black pepper to taste
- Cooking spray
- Dip of your choice to serve

Instructions:

1.   Grease 2 baking sheets with a little oil.
2.   Rinse the potatoes under cold water. Soak the potato slices in a bowl of cold water for about 15 minutes. Drain the potatoes and place on a kitchen towel in a single layer.
3.   When they are well dried, place the chips in a single layer on the prepared baking sheet.
4.   Cook the chips in batches. Place the chips on the baking sheets. Spray with cooking spray.
5.   Bake in a preheated oven at 300°F for about 15 - 20

minutes or until crisp. Turn the chips a couple of times while cooking.

6.   When chips are ready, sprinkle salt and pepper.

7.   Store in an airtight container until use.

8.   Serve chips with a dip of your choice. Suggested dip is sour cream and onion dip.

Healthy Cookie Dough Peanut Butter Protein Balls

Serves: 24

Ingredients:

- 1 ½ cups all natural drippy peanut butter or any other type of nut butter
- 1 cup protein powder
- 2 tablespoons unsweetened almond milk + extra if required
- 2 tablespoons coconut flour or extra if required
- 2 teaspoons vanilla extract
- ¼ cup chocolate chips

Instructions:

1. Add peanut butter, almond milk, coconut flour, protein powder and vanilla into a bowl and mix well.
2. Add a little more milk if the mixture is very dry or add more coconut flour if the mixture is more wet.
3. Add chocolate chips and stir again.
4. Divide the mixture into 24 equal portions. Shape each portion into a ball and place in an airtight container.
5. Refrigerate until use.

Sweet Potato Hummus

Serves: 12

Ingredients:

- 3 cups cooked garbanzo beans
- 4 tablespoons tahini
- 4 tablespoons sriracha sauce
- ¼ teaspoon paprika
- ¼ cup fresh thyme, chopped
- 1 cup sweet potato puree
- 4 tablespoons extra virgin olive oil
- ¼ teaspoon salt or to taste
- 1 teaspoon garlic powder
- 6 tablespoons fresh goat's cheese

Instructions:

1.   Add garbanzo beans, sweet potato puree, tahini, olive oil and sriracha sauce into a blender and blend until smooth.

2.   If you find the mixture very thick, then add some more olive oil.

3.   Add garlic powder, thyme and paprika and blend again.

4.   Transfer into a bowl. Sprinkle cheese on top.

5.   Cover and refrigerate until use.

6.   Serve with crackers or vegetable sticks.

Super Seed Crackers

Serves: 12 to 25 depending upon the size

Ingredients:

- ¼ cup ground flaxseeds
- ¼ cup sesame seeds
- ¼ cup brown or golden whole flaxseeds
- ¼ cup raw sunflower seeds
- 10 tablespoons water
- ¼ teaspoon salt or to taste

For everything bagel spice:

- ½ teaspoon poppy seeds
- ½ teaspoon dried onion
- ½ teaspoon sesame seeds
- ½ teaspoon dried garlic

Instructions:

1.   Prepare a baking sheet by lining it with parchment paper.

2.   Add sunflower seeds into the food processor and pulse until broken into smaller pieces. Transfer into a bowl.

3.   Add rest of the ingredients and mix well. Cover and set aside for an hour. Mix again.

4.   Transfer the mixture on to the prepared baking sheet.

5.   Bake in a preheated oven at 350°F for about 30 minutes. Switch off the oven and let it remain in the oven for an hour.

6.   Remove from the oven and cool completely.

7.   Cut into crackers of desired size.

8.   Transfer into an airtight container. It can last for a week.

Chapter 16: How you can Stay Motivated

Food that's Naturally Fatty is Nice

Fatty food tends to be so a lot better than non-fatty food. Fatty food also has a tendency to satiate faster than non-fatty food or lean food. It is crucial for maintaining your state of health. But nutritional fat doesn't mean trans-fat so steer obvious from it. Nutritional fat is essential for the metabolic operations and missing fats completely is an extremely bad and harmful idea. Consuming essential olive oil, full-fat milk products as well as fat cuts of meats will give you balance-needed nutritional fats.

Don't Go Hungry

Make certain that you simply continue to keep eating on normal times. You are able to consume 5 or 6 small meals during the day. Keep to the meals you'll be able to consume and steer clear of those you should not. As lengthy if you end up consuming just what you are permitted to consume and also the servings are common sized, in which case you needn't be worried about the amount you eat. Should you go hungry, your bloodstream sugar ranges may decrease also it would result in unnecessary effects which are completely preventable.

To be able to have the ability to take control of your urge for food and be certain that your levels of energy are fine, then you definitely really shouldn't go hungry. The recipes succumbed this book will make certain you have lots of motivation to prepare healthy and scrumptious food that may help you curb your longing for carbs.

Always Drink Plenty of Water

It is advisable to drink plenty of water to make certain the electrolyte composition within your body isn't disturbed. You have to drink 8 portions of water a minimum of and with respect to the activity level that you simply enjoy, you are able to sip much more water. You are able to have a healthy broth or non-coffee. Eco-friendly tea is a great option. Should you not drink enough water, it can cause water retentions. When bodies are well hydrated you are able to eliminate water weight.

Keep a Tabs on How Well You're Progressing

It is crucial that you're keeping a tabs on how well you're progressing. Progress doesn't just mean the load you have lost but additionally the way you've improved your wellbeing. Once each week, you need to weigh yourself and note lower your measurements too.

You need to conserve a food journal too to keep a tabs on the only thing you happen to be consuming throughout the day. Document your current working out timetable as well as any additional activities which you believe will impact your diet plan.

Avoid Sugar No Matter What

All of the sodas along with other unhealthy foods have a tendency to contain lots of added sugar which must be prevented no matter what. All foods which are manufactured include additional sugars they're at the top of calories and occasional on nutrients. You can go for non-caloric sweeteners for sweetening your drinks like Sucralose or Stevia. You will have to make sure that your daily Carbs don't exceed 3 grams of these non-caloric sweeteners. An easy rule that may help you when you're buying groceries is to steer clear of something that is available in a box.

Enjoy Your Food Intake

Meal prep is all about maintaining a healthy diet and wholesome foods that are great for you. It is important to benefit from what you're eating also it shouldn't seem like a consequence in your case. You do not need to maintain stocks of pricey pre-cooked meals or anything of this sort.

To nibble on the standard everyday ingredients and also the just have to change that you'll be making for your weight loss program is to prevent consuming carbs and sugar. You don't even need to worry when you're heading out for any meal or traveling.

You can find what you would like and eat what you would like as lengthy because it is something that the dietary plan offers. The nutritious and tasty recipes within this book will certainly assist you to benefit from the diet.

Enjoy Some Exercise

The body metabolic process will certainly improve should you enjoy some exercise. If you wish to keep your weight you have dropped away, then exercise is as essential as following a diet. You needn't always must see a fitness center to workout, apply for yoga, dancing, Zumba, swimming, brisk walking or even play an outside game like basketball or tennis. You won't just start burning calories quickly but probably begin to build muscle.

Include Protein in Your Meals

You'll need to incorporate protein in a single form or any other in your foods. Purchase an array of proteins, based on that which you want. It is possible to eat eggs, fatty meat or perhaps lean meat, sea food and shellfish, every other type of chicken too. If you want steak, you'll be able to choose a fancy marbled cut of beef.

Consume Plenty of Vegetables

You shouldn't skip or cut lower on vegetables. Vegetables are great for you and also they offer the required fiber and nutrients which are needed for you. You'll have to make certain that a minimum of 75% of the daily carb intake originates from vegetables. Which implies that you could have five to six areas of vegetables during your day. Be sure that you're getting adequate fiber every day. Fiber works well for manipulating the amounts of bloodstream sugar in your body. Fiber may also cause you to feel full which help to maintain unwanted weight.

Conclusion

Have your initial thoughts about meal prepping changed? Are you not scared of cooking anymore? I am sure that your perception about meal prepping has changed to a greater extent with this book.

It is always the fear of the unknown that dissuades us from taking on new challenges. Cooking every day was one such challenge that I kept evading for years, because I was skeptical about setting aside so much time for it. When my health started paying the price for my tendency to resort to junk eating, that's when I started doing a bit more research on healthy eating. I struck gold with meal prepping!

By now, you will definitely agree with me when I say that meal prepping can be such a gift and can help you lead a healthy lifestyle. And the best part is that you don't have to put yourself through a stringent diet to achieve your fitness goals!

Try to make the best use of the tips suggested in this book. Get the support of your family and friends! With their support, meal prepping and cooking your own meals will look like a piece of cake. Imagine how much time you can save, if your roommate also helped with prepping your meals! It may look like a daunting task to begin with! But, as you get through each week, you will realize that is one of the best things to have picked up!

You are now empowered with all the information that you need on this journey towards clean eating and a healthy lifestyle. All that is left is, for you to put that knowledge to best use. As days roll by, you will definitely see for yourself, how the quality of your life is improving by this small adjustment that you made!

When you start realizing the benefits of meal prepping, make sure to pass on the gift to others! Today's generation badly needs the gift of good health. The easiest and cheapest way to achieve that is by cooking your own meals. Try to change others' misconceptions about meal prepping and help them lead a healthy lifestyle as well.

I hope that I have converted yet another person into a meal prepping fan. I wish you all the best and I sincerely hope that you stay motivated throughout. Thank you again for purchasing this book!

Thank you!

Thank you again for purchasing this book! I hope this book was able to help you get started with these delicious recipes!

Finally, if you enjoyed this book, then I'd like to ask you for a favor, would you be kind enough to leave a review for this book on Amazon?

Leaving a review allows me to improve it and good reviews mean the world to me.

64108171R00131

Made in the USA
San Bernardino, CA
20 December 2017